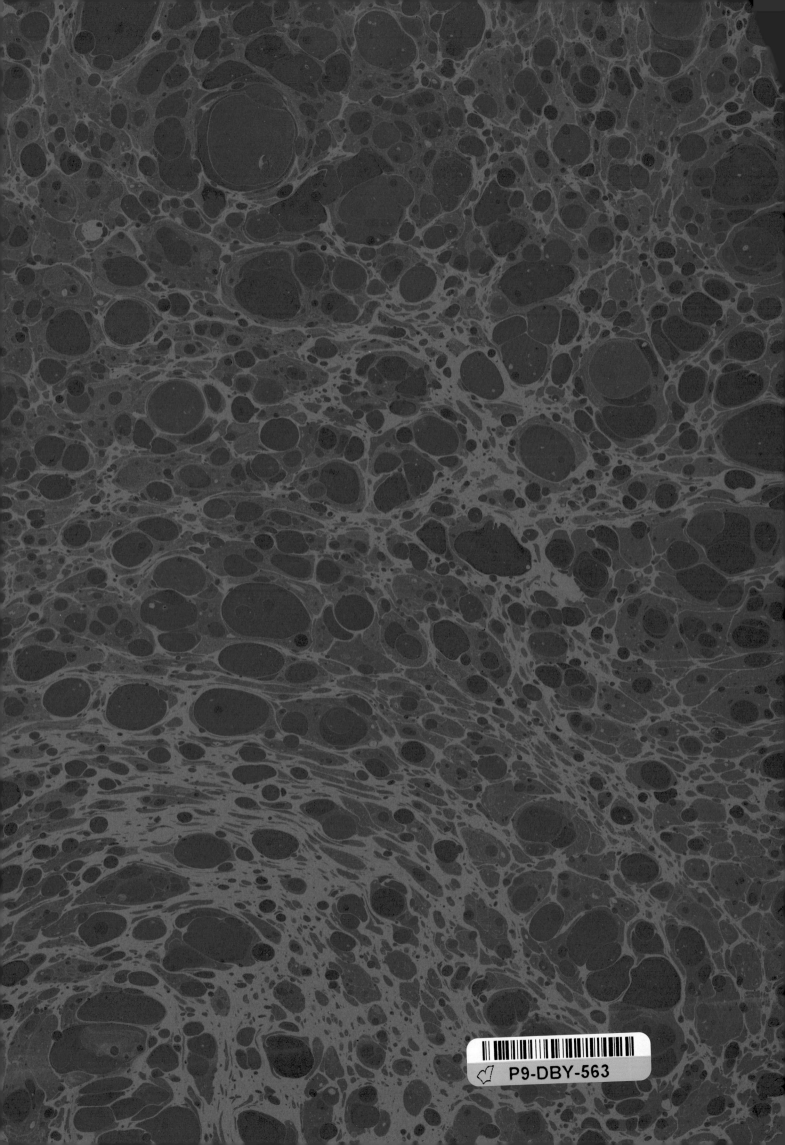

The Enchanted World

FAIRIES AND ELVES

The Enchanted World
FAIRIES AND ELVES

by the Editors of Time-Life Books

The Content

Time-Life Books · Alexandria, Virginia

Chapter One

Lands behind Enchantment's Veil

On a Midsummer Eve in Ireland long ago, a traveler rode slowly across the meadows of Connacht, heading west toward the sea on a journey that would be like none other in his life. The evening was peaceful enough. From the hedgerows drifted the scent of honeysuckle and bramble rose; on the grass beneath the horse's hoofs, a carpet of daisies winked white in the twilight. Ahead lay a forest of oak and ash, the tree trunks swathed in ground mist. And in the distance loomed the blue flanks of the Connemara Mountains.

The moon rose, a silver sickle, and the darkness deepened. Still the traveler plodded on, hearing only the sigh of the wind in the grasses and the creaking of his saddle. But as he neared the trees, he reined in, for other sounds floated on the air. Harp strings issued a shimmer

of notes; flutes described liquid, shining runs; and through the music sounded the ringing of belled bridles, heralding the approach of a great company.

A moment later, a splendid column rode out of the forest—sevenscore gold-clad knights mounted on white horses that were shod in gold and hung with golden bells. Among them was a bevy of women—princesses all, it seemed by their dress. They inclined their graceful necks when they saw the traveler, and out of gleaming eyes gave him a clear, severe, wild look that made his heart contract with longing. In and out of the mist the strangers wound, now visible, now not—of the earth and yet not of it. They moved in a nimbus of brightness, and behind them, a road leading back into the forest offered a vista of a mighty fortress, also bathed in lambent light.

The traveler never afterward could tell how long he stood transfixed, gazing at the shining company. Its riders pranced before him neither a long time nor a short one; the patterns of their time were alien to the stolid march of human hours and nights and days, just as the rhythms of their music were strange to the beat of the human heart. At last, the traveler later said, he could no longer see the riders, and he heard only an echo of a melody he never could quite recall. The gilded light and the many-towered palace in the distance were gone.

He spurred his horse and trotted to the forest's edge, where he found not a blade of grass disturbed or flattened. There was no sign of the riders or of the land that had appeared behind the trees. Although the traveler waited and listened, he saw and heard no more, only the impatient whickering of his horse.

At last he went about his business, but the rest of his life was illuminated by that one moment. When he was old, he forgot much, as old men do; but that one night he never would forget. Nodding by his fireside, he told the tale again and again. He told his son and his son's son; and each time in the telling, even when he was frail and aged, the radiance of his youth passed once more across his face and kindled his old eyes, and his listeners envied him the moonlit meadow and the night journey.

Of what the traveler had been privileged to witness, there could be no doubt. He had beheld a fairy host, riding in procession; he had been given a glimpse of a race of beings—human in form and more than human in power—that once thronged the fringes of the mortal world. And he was among the last of mortals to see such a sight, which is why his fellows envied him. In the traveler's time,

the fairies had begun to retreat from humankind. His was an era when fields were claimed from the green forests that mantled the globe, when peddlers' tracks and traders' highways reached into remote corners of the earth, when villages and cities arose in the wilderness. As the natural world was tamed, the fairies it sheltered became ever-more-elusive strangers. Yet they were not always thus.

Once, at the dreaming dawn of history—before the world was categorized and regulated by mortal minds, before solid boundaries formed between the mortal world and any other—fairies roamed freely among men, and the two races knew each other well. Yet the knowing was never straightforward, and the adventures that mortals and fairies had together were fraught with uncertainty, for fairies and humans were alien to each other.

Humans were uneasy at this time. Small creatures on a vast, wild planet, they set out to create a reassuring orderliness—to define themselves and the creatures around them, to structure countries and kingdoms, to establish hierarchies among themselves so that each would know his place and all would know the patterns that prevented anarchy.

The fairy nature, in contrast, was essentially fluid and ambiguous, marked by caprice. Fairies existed in human form, sometimes splendid and sometimes grotesque. But if they desired, fairies could also assume the shapes of deer or falcons, flames or flowers or jewels. At times, they cloaked themselves in invisibility. Although they lived on a plane that was linked to the physical world that humans knew, their realm was endowed with additional dimensions. Their kingdoms appeared and disappeared between one blink of the eye and the next, in a way that could only disturb humans: It was as if a full, complex and inexplicable life went busily on, unseen among the mortals' precariously maintained civilizations.

Fairies naturally inspired speculation. Ever curious, ever eager to name and define, mortals recorded their glimpses of them in songs and tales and poems. Naming came first, for the name of a thing was charged (as it is in some ways even now) with the essence of that thing: To know a name gave the knower some measure of control over the thing it named.

Like all else about fairies, the sources of their names were ambiguous. The words for "fairy" in Spain and in Italy were *fada* and *fata*, respectively, and these seem to have been derived from the Latin *fatum*, or "fate," in recognition of the skill fairies had in predicting and even controlling human destiny. In France, however, the similar word *fée* came from the Latin *fatare* via the Old French *féer*, meaning "to enchant." *Féer* referred to the fairies' ability to alter the world that humans saw—to cast a spell over human vision. From *féer* came not only *fée* but the English word "Faerie," which encompassed both the art of enchantment and the whole realm in which fairies had their being. "Fairy" and "fay"—other derivatives of the parent word—referred only to the individual creatures.

The other common English term for an individual fairy was "elf," and this derived not from Latin but from the Nordic and Teutonic languages, reaching England with invasions from the Continent. In Scandinavia, the word for "elves" was *alfar*, which – appropriately, since fairies were tied to the things of the earth – had to do with mountains and water.

Mortals used these various terms interchangeably to describe a broad range of elusive beings. Mindful of the fairies' nature, they most often referred to the race as a whole by epithets – the Gentry or the Good People or the Mothers' Blessing, and the like. In those days, using a creature's true name without permission implied a threat – unwise in the case of fairies, whose reactions were unpredictable and whose powers were great.

For the purpose of classification, however, the entire race could be roughly divided into a peasantry and an aristocracy. The peasants were solitary fairies, descendants of the spirits who at the beginning of time ensouled all nature. They were guardians of tree and field, of forest pool and mountain stream. Although they shared in some powers of Faerie, such as the ability to become invisible or to appear in various shapes, solitary fairies were wild creatures, and their meetings with mortals were relatively rare compared with those of their grand relatives. The presence of a solitary fairy was most often announced not by a direct sighting but by evidence of the creature's activity: the bending of grass as a fairy passed invisibly over it, soughing sounds in tree branches, glittering frost patterns etched on windowpanes.

The aristocracy of Faerie was a different matter. Known as trooping fairies, these beings were descended, it was popularly thought, from ancient, vanquished gods. They were a powerful race who dwelled in kingdoms underground or across the deepest seas; to mortals they were objects of infinite desire and sometimes infinite fear. The *alfar* of Scandinavia were believed to be divided into good and bad branches: the Liosálfar, or Light Elves, who were air dwellers; and the Döckálfar, or Dark Elves, whose kingdoms were beneath the ground. The Scots made the same distinction: Their fairy bands were called the Seelie – or Blessed – Court and the Unseelie Court, the latter often being thought of as the vengeful ghosts of dead mortals.

No such division was made in Wales or Ireland: There the trooping fairies – companies like the one the traveler had seen in the meadows of Connacht – were taken as a whole in all their complex manifestations. In Wales they were called the Tylwyth Teg – the Fair Family. In Ireland they were known as the Daoine Side – the Dwellers of the Fairy Mounds, for it was under those softly swelling, grassy knolls that many of their palaces were hidden.

Ireland, in fact, provides the most complete accounts of the trooping fairies and their kind: Irish tales and songs trace the history of these fairies back thousands of years, to a time before the boundaries between their world and the mortal one became dangerous to cross, before mortals grew to fear entrapment in the lands of the fairies, and before the love that could exist between mortal and fairy turned to hopeless yearning.

At that time, the island had not yet been

completely formed and defined. Its hills and lakes and streams were still without names and identities. But mortals were present in numbers. According to the histories, Ireland had been settled by a people called the Firbolg, who were beginning to tame the rich wilderness.

On the first day of May one year, the sky to the north of the island was darkened by a cloud that spread across the rolling hills and blotted out the sun. It gathered around the peaks of the mountain of Conmaicne Réin, in the very heart of Ireland, and hung in the air for three days. When the mist thinned and drifted out to sea, troops of glittering warriors wound in columns down the mountain, drove away the people of the Firbolg and took the island for themselves.

The fairy warriors had come from enchanted islands at the top of the world, traveling to this green and pleasant land in the dark cloud that had settled around Conmaicne Réin. They were called by humans Tuatha Dé Danann, which meant "the people of the goddess Danu" – a fertility goddess. (The title may have come to them because of their elfin power over the growth of crops.) They were famed, in the words of an early scribe, as "the most handsome and delightful company, the fairest of form, the most distinguished in their equipment and apparel, and their skill in music and playing, the most gifted in mind and temperament that ever came to Ireland." Their power was great, for they possessed magic talismans: a spear and sword no enemy could survive, and a caldron that was never empty of food.

How long the Tuatha reigned nobody knows. But some time in an antiquity older than the granite of the Irish mountains, they were conquered, despite their talismans, by new and mortal invaders, ancestors of the Gaels, who were to rule the island. The Tuatha took refuge in invisibility. Some built kingdoms within the hollow hills or beneath the lakes of Ireland, Scotland and Wales, and some made their homes on islands far across the western seas. They hid their kingdoms with walls that were invisible except to themselves and impenetrable to most mortals.

That was the beginning of the retreat of the Tuatha and the time when they gained the name Daoine Side. But their final disappearance would not come for hundreds and hundreds of years. Meanwhile, these heroic beings pursued their wars and loves, generally unseen by the humans who had conquered them.

During those centuries, fairy and mortal – though separated – were bound in a network of needs and desires. Linked by the world of stream and sea, of leaf and tree and field, the two races reached out to each other, in defiance of their alien natures. Again and again, in the comradeship of arms or in the bright fires of love, the beings of Faerie ventured into the mortal world. Again and again, mortals set out on journeys that carried them unknowing across the boundaries of Faerie, and their adventures were curious indeed.

For the seagirt Irish, each ocean voyage was uncertain. The waters of the Irish Sea and the North Atlantic were speckled with strange and shifting islands, as the

The golden company's overlord

The High King of the Tuatha Dé Danann – heroic fairies of Ireland's distant past – was the bearer of many titles and the source of many legends. He was styled the Father of All, as well as Lord of Knowledge and Sun of All the Sciences; his chief title, Dagda, meant the "Good God."

The term Dagda did not refer to the elfin lord's virtue: Legends of gluttony and savagery clustered around him. Instead, it meant that he shone in every sphere and was the most powerful among that race of powerful fairies. He had a battle club that could slay nine men with a single blow. He owned a magic caldron that never was empty of food. And the music of his harp could cause laughter or grief, or give the gift of sleep.

When his fairy host left the surface of the earth and took up residence under the hills of Ireland, the Dagda created four separate kingdoms and gave each to a different son. But this mightiest of fairies remained sovereign over all.

13

Irish *immrama*—voyage tales—record. Adventurers told of sighting such islands as one of cat-headed men and another of men with dogs' heads; one with a fountain that yielded milk, ale and wine; one of giant horses; and one that turned anything cast on one side white, and anything cast on the other black.

It was hard to tell in those days whether a sea voyage would go on in a normal, uneventful way, or whether the fierce wind and tides of the North would drive the little boats off course and across an invisible barrier into the realm of Faerie, where adventures would begin, as they did for a prince named Teigue. His story was this:

Teigue was the heir of an early lord of Munster, in the west of Ireland, and he took to the sea on a voyage of rescue and revenge. A marauder named Cathmann, with a fleet of nine ships, had invaded Teigue's lands, laid waste the fields, burned the villages and departed for his own stronghold—an island off the coast of Spain—taking as captives Teigue's wife, Liban, and two of his brothers.

Teigue was left with forty warriors, one captive from Cathmann's band and a fierce determination to deliver his family. He caused a currach—a stout ship—to be built. It had strong masts and broad-bladed oars; and the frame was covered, the story says, with hard, red leather made from the hides of forty oxen.

On a bitter morning in March, they launched the little ship at Kerry Head, sliding her over the pebbles of the shore and into the grip of cresting seas. With their oars flashing, the Irishmen drove forward into wind and icy rain, and it was not long before Teigue and his forty warriors—and the captive enemy, whom they had taken along to guide them—were out of sight of the cliffs of Munster.

They sailed for a month, seeing little on the limitless and rolling sea except the sleek brown heads of inquisitive seals and the flash of leaping fish; from time to time they heard the blowing of whales. Twice they put in at unnamed islands to rest and reprovision. Then came a space of six weeks when they made no landfall at all and traveled in a cloud of mist that was broken only occasionally by streaks of pale and watery sunlight.

The men grew hushed and drawn. The captive guide, chained in the bow, squinted anxiously ahead, but he had lost his bearings in the fog. At last he said hopelessly, "We are adrift, drifting with the tide and I know not where it will take us."

Immediately after he spoke, a howling wind arose in the distance and tore across the sea toward them like a falcon stooping on its prey. The sea swelled high above the masts in roaring mountains that smashed icy torrents across the bow. Gasping under the onslaught, the men pulled at their oars with cold-stiffened fingers. As Teigue shouted encouragement, they brought the boat around into the wind and held her there safely, throughout the day and the screaming night that followed.

Morning came at last, and the gale died. The sun rose, scattering diamonds across the surface of the sea. The men raised the currach's sails and headed west, and the sun played on their backs as they rested.

A benison from the Blessed Court

Although their feelings toward mortals were complex, fairies of the early days sometimes acted with great kindness, as this tale tells:

Once a Scottish knight dared to scorn the love of a woman who had witching powers. In her fury at the insult, she transformed him: Where the young man had been lay a reptilian creature, scaled and cold. Trapped in the loathsome body, the knight huddled by a tree for months.

On the Eve of Samain in that year, when the full moon rose and the fields shone in its light, the pitiful beast heard the sound of flutes and trumpets. It raised its heavy head and saw the glitter of the Seelie Court —the heroic fairies of Scotland—as they wound in procession through the hills, blessing the farmers' crops. All across the countryside the bright company wandered and at last came to the place where the knight lay in his bestial guise.

The Seelie Queen paused in her riding. She dismounted and drew near him, signaling her fairies to ride on. As their music faded into the distance, she sat on the grass and drew the head of the bewitched knight into her lap. She stroked the scales and softly sang.

All the while, the knight lay motionless. The moon set, the stars dimmed, and the eastern horizon began to glow. Then the skin that covered the knight split and tore and at last fell away, so that the young man emerged clean and whole. He started to thank the Seelie Queen, but before he could speak, she faded into the light of morning, returning invisibly to her kingdom underground.

Soon they saw in the distance a coastline. They steered for it, and at length the currach slid quietly into an estuary of green water so clear that the voyagers could see the silvery sands of the bottom and watch the darting of the scarlet salmon that played there. The shore on either side was fringed with trees, and from their midst poured the carols of unknown birds.

Teigue and his men made for shore and together pulled the currach up to dry on the shingle. Then they entered the wood.

The travelers knew at once that this was no ordinary place. In Munster, spring had just begun; the earth was bare and hard there, and the trees were black. Here, however, the trees were thick with leaves and heavy with fruit. Their branches swayed gently, although no wind stirred, and they seemed to listen as the intruders passed beneath them. All were trees sacred to the Irish from ancient times, so revered that anyone who cut them might forfeit his life. Some were venerable and mighty oaks, worshipped since time began and sentient still: Oaks wailed when they were cut. Apple trees—fertile guardians of immortality—grew in abundance, laden with scarlet globes. And among them stood many hazel trees, heavy with the clusters of yellow nuts that in Ireland sometimes bestow all the world's wisdom on the mortal lucky enough to eat them.

After the men had walked some little distance, the wood thinned and became sunny again and parklike. Then the travelers found themselves at the verge of the wood, looking into the country that it guarded. They laughed and exclaimed at the sight that met their eyes.

Stretching out to the rim of the sky was a wide, smooth plain, cloaked in the green and white of flowering clover. Breaking the expanse were three grassy hills, each guarded by a high-walled palace. The men set out for the nearest one. At its marble ramparts, they met a blithe and shining lady. She seemed to expect the travelers and to trust them, for she called Teigue by name and sent him with his men to the hill beyond, where the scene was repeated.

The travelers came to the third of the hills and, as they had been instructed, passed through the mighty arched gate of the castle there and entered the courtyard. At its center grew a wide-spreading apple tree, its branches white with blossoms— and also laden with fruit.

From among the white blossoms drifted a woman like a flower, her hair resembling silvered petals. She regarded the mortals with a calm gaze and said Teigue's name. Care fell from him at the sound of her voice, and he listened with a calm that matched her own as she told these things:

She said that she was a daughter—called Clíodna Fair Hair—of the Tuatha Dé Danann and that the island was her own. She said that the fruit of her apple tree was of such power that mortals who ate it would never hunger and would always be drawn to her lands. And she warned them that when a day passed in her realm, though it seemed but a day, a year passed in the mortal world, so that Teigue was reminded of the quest he had undertaken.

Then the fairy told Teigue that she would give three gifts to aid him on his quest. The first was a guide to the place of battle. The guide comprised three birds she summoned from the branches of the apple tree: one blue with a crimson head, one scarlet with a head of green and one of many colors whose head shone gold. The second gift the fairy gave was an emerald chalice. It would guard Teigue's life as long as he kept it by him, she said. And the last gift was this: She told Teigue what the manner of his death would finally be, so he knew that the time for it had not yet come. She told him, too, that she herself would be with him on his last day, on the banks of the Boyne River, when a wild hart would gore and kill him.

After she had spoken, those two — the mortal and the fairy — smiled gravely at each other, for such was the Fair Hair's power that she had armored Teigue against fear, although the men with him shuffled anxiously and whispered among themselves. But they followed Teigue willingly when he left the court and, with the fairy beside him, crossed the flowering plain again and made his way through the enchanted wood to the currach.

The water whispered around the ship's bow as it headed down the estuary. High above the masts, the three birds rode the bright air and sang without cease. On the bank stood the fairy, arrow-straight and starbright. She neither moved nor spoke again, but she watched Teigue steadily.

When the currach reached open water and gathered speed, Teigue turned to look a last time and thus saw the sheet of mist that rose from the water at the island shore and crept swiftly up the banks, curling around the trees and around the figure of

Mistress for a Fairy King

In the era when fairies and mortals lived side by side in the world, an Irish lord named Eochaid gambled away his beautiful wife, Etain, to a ruler of elfin lands. This is how it happened:

Etain won the attention of Midhir — a King among the Tuatha Dé Danann — who wooed her in secret, promising to take her to his invisible realm. Swayed by his singing, she agreed, but she said that her husband must give her leave. Midhir bided his time for a year; then he appeared at Eochaid's stronghold.

"Who are you?" asked the lord.

"Midhir of Bri Leith."

"Why have you come?"

"To play at *fidchell* with you."

Fidchell was a game like chess, played on a silver board with golden men, and Eochaid prided himself on his skill at it. He agreed to play, but only for a stake. Midhir smiled and set it: fifty dark horses with blood red heads. Midhir lost, and by the next dawn, Eochaid had his horses. Then they played again for a richer stake, which included fifty fiery boats and fifty swords with golden hilts. Again Midhir lost, and again Eochaid got his booty. They decided to play a third time. When Eochaid asked the stake, Midhir said, "Whatever the winner names." Eochaid greedily agreed. This time Midhir won. He set the stake: his arm around Etain and a kiss from her lips. Eochaid hesitated, but in honor he had no choice. He promised to deliver Etain in one month's time. When Midhir arrived on the appointed day, he found Eochaid and Etain in the castle courtyard, surrounded by Eochaid's warriors. But the ranks parted as the King strode through. Midhir shifted his weapons from his right hand to his left and put his right arm around Etain. Effortlessly, the two rose into the air, higher and higher, until they were mere specks, two swans flying across the countryside, toward Midhir's bright land.

Thus began a war between mortal and fairy, but Midhir kept his mortal mistress.

Voyaging in search of an enemy, the Irish chieftain Teigue came upon a fairy isle.

Its Queen welcomed him and sent him on his way with magical gifts: bright-plumaged birds to guide him and an emerald chalice to guard him from harm.

the fairy until at last it blanketed even the tops of the tallest oaks.

The mist eventually dispersed into coiling white ribbons drifting on the water's surface; then even these ribbons disappeared, and where the island had been was only empty sea. And the red-sided currach, her canvas billowing with Faerie wind, sailed southward. Above her masts, the three birds flashed and tumbled and sang their dancing harmonies. In the boat, the men of Munster lay entranced.

They awoke only when the singing ceased, and the birds had become three bright specks in the northern sky, heading for home. At once, the currach grated on a beach, her sails slack. The travelers were at the edge of a narrow loch that pierced the shore of a harsh, pine-covered country. Across the waters of the loch were the ramparts of a wooden stronghold; from its tower hung the pennon of the pirate Cathmann, abductor of Teigue's wife and enslaver of his brothers. The Munstermen had arrived at the place of battle.

Leaving his company to guard the currach, Teigue armed himself and set out to reconnoiter. As he walked along the sand, he heard his name called softly across the water. A ragged ferryman, pulling hard at the oars of a shabby boat, approached and beached his craft. It was Teigue's brother Eoghan, brought to this humble pass after a year of captivity under Cathmann.

Eoghan's news was good: Teigue's wife was safe but a prisoner, and Cathmann meant soon to take her for his own, having been delayed only by her pleading. Teigue had arrived in a time of conspiracy, for two of Cathmann's kinsmen were armed, and Eoghan as well as Teigue's brother Airnelach had joined them in secret. Eoghan spent some time describing Cathmann's defenses. Then he ferried Teigue and his men to the opposite shore, where Cathmann's castle stood. Among the pine trees there, rebellious kinsmen of the pirate hid with their forces.

Thus it came about that the Irish Prince took his revenge on the outlander, not with a small force of forty men, but with a company of 700. The warriors stormed the fortress that night, when Cathmann and his men had drunk deep after their feasting. It was a savage battle, and in the end, the Irish put the castle to the torch. Amid the flickering light of the flames and crowds of sweating, shouting men, Teigue and Cathmann fought alone, and the Munsterman took blow after blow from the pirate until he was driven to his knees. He carried the fairy's emerald talisman, however, and it gave him the strength to rise once more and strike his enemy's head from his shoulders. Teigue bore thirty wounds, but he did not die.

His death came many years later, long after Teigue and his wife and brothers had returned to Ireland. He lived in peace until the day that a white hart attacked him on the banks of the Boyne and the maiden from the enchanted isle appeared before him once again, as she had promised years before.

In none of their tellings of the venture could Teigue or his men ever identify the point on the ocean where they had crossed the borders of their own world and entered the realm of Faerie. They did not know: The borders of the other world were ever-shifting and transitory. It was significant, however, that the moment of crossing came when the currach was adrift – off course and traveling in no direction that could be defined. It was significant, too, that the first event of the crossing was a sample of chaos in the shape of a storm. The fairy world was in some ways the antithesis of the world of mortals, and things of Faerie had a natural affinity for the indeterminate and the undefinable. To relax the mortal grasp of order was to invite passage between the two worlds.

In those days, despite the brave efforts of the human mind, the world was full of uncertainties. It was not just the unknown wilderness that frightened mortals – the uncharted seas that lapped the land, the looming mountains and the forests that encroached on field and village and castle. The natural world was dangerous enough, to be sure. But even greater uncertainties lay close at hand: Mortal time and mortal space were seamed with cracks that served as doorways to places where human rules were meaningless.

It is not surprising, then, that mortals set great store by definition. Because things could be easily understood in terms of what they were not, people thought about their world in terms of pairs of opposites. The seasons, for instance, were winter, when nature slept, and summer, when the earth bloomed; correspondingly, the hours separated easily into dark night and bright day.

But what of the times that were neither one thing nor its opposite, and thus free of the bonds of classification? What of dawn and dusk, which were neither night nor day? What of noon and midnight? What of the nights between the seasons – October 31, or Samain Eve (later called Allhallows Eve), and April 30, Beltane Eve (later called May Day Eve)? On those nights, the year's most mysterious and wonder-filled, all mortal rules were suspended, and chaos reigned. They were the times when passage between the mortal world and other worlds was most free.

It was the same with space: Mortals liked to define it. They made countries and shires and townships and castle walls and farm fences, all in the interest of delineating the space they inhabited. The matter of boundaries was so important that throughout Europe, in a springtime ceremony called Beating the Bounds, all the known limits of local space were redefined, sometimes by whipping the borders of property with hazel twigs and sometimes by using the twigs on young boys as they were sent around the limits of a territory, thus passing on the knowledge of generations. But what of the dividing lines themselves: the streams that marked a territory, the shores of the sea, the verges of lakes, the fords of rivers, the crossroads, fences, walls and thresholds? These, being neither one place nor another, served as portals to the world of Faerie.

So people were alert and careful at borderline times and places, knowing that strange encounters were possible. The spirits of the dead roamed free, for one thing: An Irishman

While coursing a milk white, red-eyed stag—colors proclaiming its fairy nature—the Welsh Prince Pwyll crossed into another world. There waited Arawn, King of Annwfn, the enchanted land, who stood in need of just such an ally as this valiant mortal.

who ventured out on the Eves of Samain or Beltane never looked behind him when he heard the sound of footsteps; those were the footsteps of dead men, as he well knew. In Wales it was said that a ghost sat on every stile. (Stiles—sets of steps that allow people to climb over boundary fences where there is no gate—were in-between, or borderline, places.) Witches flew on the borderline nights. And the future was revealed: Those who waited on English church porches might hear a voice recite the names of all who would die in the coming year. On the nights before the seasons changed, the fairies traveled abroad, their power at its peak. The trooping fairies rode in festive processions known as fairy rades. Often their purpose was benevolent: Scotland's Seelie Court rode forth to bless the mortals' crops, it was said.

An age would come when humans feared what fairies might do on these borderline nights. But before the races drew apart, people stole into the fields on festival eves in hopes of seeing fairies dance on the greensward and hearing their seductive music, or of watching a door open in a hillside to reveal the gleaming lights of the kingdom within, or of witnessing a splendid procession. In those easy days, too, people did not hesitate, as they later would, to venture on journeys that took them into unknown territories and across borders they might not even recognize. Teigue's ocean voyage was a journey of that kind, and so was the venture of a Welsh lord named Pwyll, who went on a hunt that changed his life.

Pwyll was Prince of Dyfed, in the southwest of Wales. One day in autumn, when the air was crisp and cool, his thoughts turned to hunting. With his men and hounds, he headed through the forested hills toward a glen on the River Cuch, where, he had heard, fine stags were to be found. The company rode all day to

reach the re-
gion. That night,
they camped; and before
the sun rose the next morning,
Pwyll roused the men and hounds for the
hunt. With the hounds snuffling and
dancing around the horses' hoofs, the
company set off into the depths of the
forest, just at first light. In a short time,
the hounds picked up a scent and charged
off at great speed, baying and yelping as
they tore through the underbrush.

Pwyll gave a shout and followed as
close as he could, racing far ahead
of his own men, heedless of the rough
ground and the whipping branches. For a
moment, the hounds disappeared from his
view, but he soon caught up with them;
they were clustered together and growl-
ing at the edge of a small clearing. Pwyll
reined in his lathered horse and took
stock. In the clearing was a pack of strange
hounds piled upon the twitching body of
a stag they had just brought down. These
were like no hounds Pwyll had ever seen.
They were glittering white, with ears
and eyes of ruby red. He waited a moment, but no one was in sight and the
forest was silent. He had no idea where he
was. With a shrug, he spurred his horse
into the clearing, drove off the strange
hounds and set his own dogs to feeding on
the body of the stag.

After a few moments, he looked up to find himself observed – with contempt – by a tall man, dressed in hunting clothes, who sat astride a fine dappled horse.

"I will not greet you, stranger," said this man. "It is a lout's discourtesy to take the prize of another man's kill."

Pwyll stiffened with chagrin. "What is your country, stranger?" he asked.

"Annwfn," said the gray-clad hunter. Annwfn meant "not world." Pwyll now knew that somewhere – when he lost his way as he coursed the stag, or when he entered the clearing – he had crossed the border into Faerie. "I am Arawn, King of Annwfn," said the huntsman.

Pwyll said, "Only tell me how I may clear my honor with you, Lord."

"This way," said Arawn. "Go in my shape to Annwfn, and reign there in my place for a year and a day. You shall have all my powers during that time, and the dearest woman in the world to warm your bed. I will be in your shape in your own lands, ruling in your place. At the end of the year, you will fight my enemy for me. He is Havgan, whose lands march with my own and who fights me for them every year. If you fight successfully, I will meet you in this place once more."

Pwyll agreed, and the two rode together to the far edge of the clearing. Arawn pointed to where a palace glimmered in the distance. "There is my country," he said. As the mortal spurred his mount, the Fairy King added, "If you would live, strike Havgan only one blow, and strike to kill. A second blow restores him."

Then Arawn rode away. But before he entered the forest, he turned and raised his hand. Pwyll gave a start, for the man who waved was himself. He looked at his hands on the reins. They were the narrow hands of Arawn.

Clothed in the stranger's skin, Pwyll rode forward into Annwfn, looking about him with great curiosity. The path wound through green fields laced by shining streams. At its end lay a castle with many turrets, their roof tiles glinting in the sunshine, their pennants snapping in the breeze. The castle gates were open, and as Pwyll entered, grooms came to draw off his boots and take his horse. Gold-clad knights, young and merry, clustered around him, chattering about the hunt as they walked into the hall. And Pwyll saw that Arawn was beloved in his own world.

In the hall, fires crackled, and long tables were laid for feasting. Arawn's wife awaited Pwyll there. The King had not lied: She was the loveliest lady Pwyll had ever seen. Her hair shone gold in the firelight, and her flesh was so translucent that when she drank wine from his cup, Pwyll imagined he could see the red liquid flowing down her throat. All during the evening of feasting she stayed by Pwyll's side, talking affectionately and smiling up at him. It was clear that Arawn's lady loved her husband, and Pwyll answered in kind. But when the courtiers at last withdrew and the couple went together to the bedchamber, Pwyll lay in bed with his face to the wall and made no sound or move, even when the lady curled against him. Although he was clothed in another man's skin, he would not take that man's wife.

Matters continued thus for the appointed year: Each day was spent in hunting

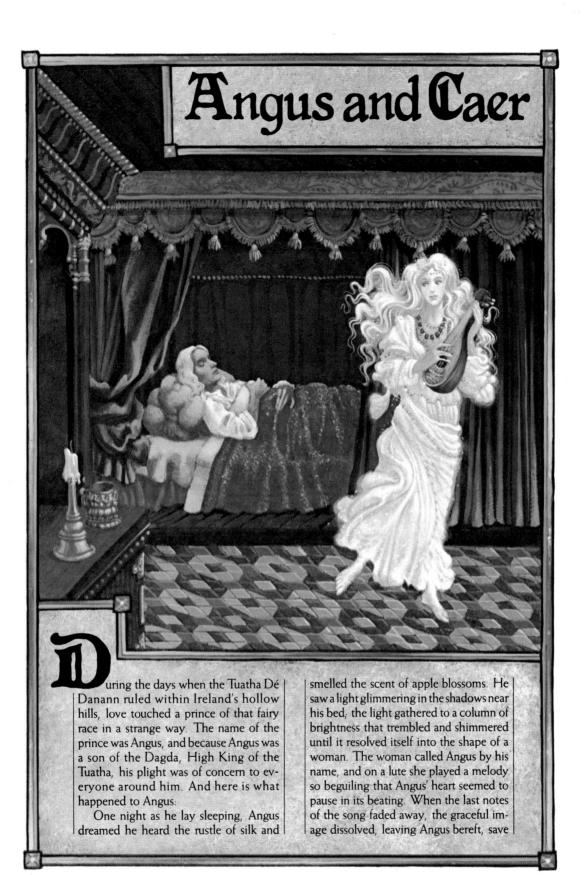

Angus and Caer

During the days when the Tuatha Dé Danann ruled within Ireland's hollow hills, love touched a prince of that fairy race in a strange way. The name of the prince was Angus, and because Angus was a son of the Dagda, High King of the Tuatha, his plight was of concern to everyone around him. And here is what happened to Angus:

One night as he lay sleeping, Angus dreamed he heard the rustle of silk and smelled the scent of apple blossoms. He saw a light glimmering in the shadows near his bed; the light gathered to a column of brightness that trembled and shimmered until it resolved itself into the shape of a woman. The woman called Angus by his name, and on a lute she played a melody so beguiling that Angus' heart seemed to pause in its beating. When the last notes of the song faded away, the graceful image dissolved, leaving Angus bereft, save

for the lingering scent of apple blossoms.

Each night thereafter, the same image appeared in Angus' dream, perfectly desirable and infinitely remote. A whole year passed in this fashion, and as night succeeded night, the Prince drew away from his fellows. He grew weak and pale because he was pining for the woman in his dream; Angus was dying of the longing that the Irish people called "love in absence."

When the Dagda learned of his son's illness, he commanded that Ireland be searched for the maiden who haunted Angus' dream.

For many months the armies of the Tuatha combed the hidden regions of the country, and at long last, at a place in the Galty Mountains that was called the Lake of the Dragon's Mouth, they found what they had been seeking. They took the ailing Prince in a chariot along the forest-shrouded mountain track that led to the place.

Peace and beauty reigned there. The lake

was a sheet of still water that mirrored sailing clouds and was framed by green reeds. And before long Prince Angus saw something else. Among the reeds drifted a crowd of silent fairy women, clothed in fluttering draperies as white as apple blossoms.

The women moved in pairs, and each pair was linked by a chain made of silver. One among them walked alone, taller than all the others, and that one wore a chain made of gold. She smiled gravely at Angus, but she spoke not a word.

"This is the woman," said the Prince.

"She is Caer Ibormeith, daughter of Ethal Anubal, who is King of the host of Connacht," said one of the Tuatha Kings. "It is to him we must go to ask for her, and the asking will be hard."

This was so. Ethal Anubal refused even to speak to them, and in the end, the Dagda and his armies stormed Ethal's fortress.

In the fierce battle that followed, the ar-

mies of the Dagda killed sixty warriors and made Ethal the King their captive. As the price of his freedom, the Dagda demanded Ethal's daughter for Angus.

But Ethal would not give her. Ethal did not have her for the giving, he said, because Caer's power was far greater than his. She lived with her maidens in a woman's form one year and in a swan's form the next, and her nature was such that only as a swan would she receive a man.

"And when will she be a swan again?" asked one of Ethal's captors.

Then Ethal told them what they must do: Angus must go the Lake of the Dragon's Mouth at the next Samain – that is, Allhallows – and himself ask Caer, who would be in swan form, for her hand.

When the time came, Angus and the Dagda journeyed once more to the Lake of the Dragon's Mouth. And there among the reeds Angus saw not young women but pairs

of cloud-white swans, linked each to each by silver chains.

In the midst of the swans was one that wore a golden chain and swam alone, gazing at her reflection in the water. Angus spoke to her from the shore.

"Who calls me?" asked the swan.

"Angus calls," the Prince replied.

"I will come to you," said the swan, "if you will swear on your honor that I always may return to my lake."

"I swear it," said the Prince.

Majestically, the swan glided to where An-gus stood at the verge of the lake. Then the Dagda and his attendants saw Angus the Prince no more. Instead, a mighty swan spread its wings above the swan in the water, hiding her from view.

The two great birds—the one that had been Angus and the one that was Caer—swam three times around the lake together, then took flight, rising into the sky in easy spirals.

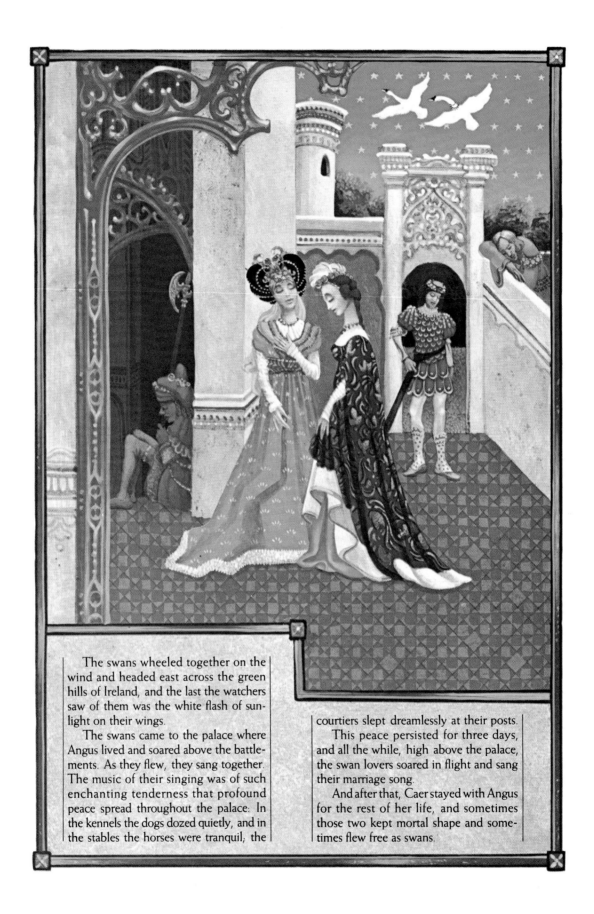

The swans wheeled together on the wind and headed east across the green hills of Ireland, and the last the watchers saw of them was the white flash of sunlight on their wings.

The swans came to the palace where Angus lived and soared above the battlements. As they flew, they sang together. The music of their singing was of such enchanting tenderness that profound peace spread throughout the palace: In the kennels the dogs dozed quietly, and in the stables the horses were tranquil; the courtiers slept dreamlessly at their posts.

This peace persisted for three days, and all the while, high above the palace, the swan lovers soared in flight and sang their marriage song.

And after that, Caer stayed with Angus for the rest of her life, and sometimes those two kept mortal shape and sometimes flew free as swans.

and feasting and making merry with the Queen of Annwfn; and each night, Pwyll turned his body to the wall beside the bed and spoke not a word.

At the end of the year, Pwyll armed himself and went forth to do battle with Havgan. Arawn's knights rode with him to the place, which was a ford that bridged a stream separating the two fairy territories.

Across the stream waited Havgan, a heavy, pale-eyed man surrounded by his followers. When Havgan saw his enemy, he raised the lance he bore and cried, "All who hear, listen well. This is single combat between two Kings to decide who rules these lands. Let none but us meet in battle." His followers and Arawn's drew back, and the two Kings wheeled their chargers into position. Then Havgan nodded and lowered his lance, and the warriors charged directly at each other, meeting with a mighty crash at the center of the ford. Havgan cried out, and shouts rose from the stream banks. Pwyll's lance had struck the boss of his foe's shield, splitting it and piercing the enemy's armor.

The Fairy King slumped forward on his horse's neck, then fell, his lifeblood staining the waters of the ford.

The light began to dwindle in his eyes as he regarded the man in Arawn's place. At that moment, he seemed to recognize Pwyll through the veil of Arawn's flesh. "I had no quarrel with you," he said. "Since you have begun the kill, however, finish my pain and give me death."

But Pwyll heeded Arawn's final words. "Let him who wishes strike another blow," he replied, "for I will not do it."

Then Havgan cried to his men, "I can no longer maintain you!" The blood ran red from his mouth, and he died in the shallow waters of the ford. Pwyll looked across the fallen King to the warriors on the opposite bank and said, "Decide among yourselves now who will follow me and end this struggle." And one by one, Havgan's warriors came to him and did him homage.

Thus the fairy kingdoms were united under Arawn's rule by Pwyll. The next day, the mortal left the palace and the lady behind and rode alone to the clearing as he and Arawn had agreed.

The Fairy King in the mortal's shape was there before him. "I have ruled your lands in Dyfed well," said he.

"I have cleansed the stain of my honor," Pwyll replied. The two crossed the clearing and saluted each other. Then each rode toward his own lands, and as they passed the verges of the clearing, each returned to his own flesh.

When Arawn reached his palace, his household greeted him as always, for they had never been aware of his absence. But his lady—though she bantered with him gaily as she always had, and drank wine from his cup—seemed withdrawn. After the revelries, Arawn went to their chamber; he drew her into his arms at once, for he had missed her sorely, but she stiffened and turned her head away in silence.

"What is this?" said Arawn.

"Why do you caress me now, when for a year you would not touch me?" she said with sadness.

"Of course I have touched you," answered Arawn the King.

No mortal could tell where Faerie lay: The curtain of invisibility that cloaked its towering mountains and turreted castles lifted only at the whim of the fairies themselves.

She shook her head. Arawn was silent, pondering the fidelity of the mortal who had taken his place. At last he said gently, "Forgive me, Lady, but I have been far from you for this year past." And he told her all that had happened.

When he had done so, the lady said, "That was a faithful friend you had, who denied himself for you."

"So I think," Arawn replied.

"And well you might," his lady said, but she laughed as she spoke, and all was well.

That was how a fairy and a mortal became faithful friends for all their lives. They hunted together in the mortal world and in Annwfn; they sent each other gifts of hawks and hounds and horses. When Pwyll's valor became known, he often was called Head of Annwfn, rather than Prince of Dyfed, and he found a fairy wife of his own, whose name was Rhiannon.

Such bridging friendships and easy traffic between the mortal and the fairy realms were rare even in the world's young age, and they would become rarer still as the centuries wore away. As the realm of humankind expanded and that of nature receded, Faerie receded as well, to become something rich and strange that was glimpsed only on infrequent occasions or from far away.

It would happen, say, that a sailor would glance idly over his ship's side and see, as in a rock pool, mountains mantled with tall trees and crowned by turreted palaces. In the green depths he might spy shepherds tending their flocks or horsemen riding to the hunt. His ship's shadow would cross the landscape as cloud shadows cross earthly fields and hills, and the

creatures below would turn curious faces up to look, and perhaps they would meet his gaze. Off the coast of Scotland, it was said, there was such a kingdom, sometimes called Lochlann, and sometimes Sorcha. (The Scots said that the children of its King were seals – or selkies – when in the sea and human when they came on land. Their fate was always to be lonely. They could not be content in either place, because "it is given to them that their sea-longing shall be land-longing, and their land-longing shall be sea-longing.")

On the wild western coasts of Ireland and Norway, people who paused to observe the crimson path of the setting sun might see misty islands rising from the waves. They knew these belonged to Faerie, for they could see the sun make fiery lights on the windows of the castles there. But the islands always disappeared into the sea again. The Irish called them the Isles of the Blest and gave them many names. Tir na n'Og, or the Land of the Young, was one; Tirn Aill, or the Other World, was another. Off the Welsh coast was Ynis Gwydrin, or the Island of Glass, so called because the palaces there were made of glass and shone like crystal.

And on the land, fairy kingdoms were hidden in grassy mounds that on Allhallows Eve might open or even rise into the air on pillars to reveal the glittering palaces within; the mounds existed both in Ireland and in Scotland.

If these elusive places could be reached, a wistful traveler remarked, they would be proved to be filled with luminous intensity, their sun more golden and moon more silver than those of the mortal world, their flowers more fragrant and their fruit more sweet. "Everything in Faerie is better by this one wonderful degree," he said, "and it is by this betterness that you will know that you are there."

It was no wonder that some adventurers among the world's youth forsook their own realm and chose to stay within the boundaries of Faerie. A man named Loegaire, the son of a King of Connacht, did that. Loegaire had fought in battle beside a Fairy King named Fiachna and loved that King's country so well that he severed every human tie to stay within it, thereby breaking his own father's heart.

Another such adventurer was the Irish chieftain O'Donoghue, a warrior so valiant that even the Tuatha sang his praises. O'Donoghue left his stronghold one May Day morning and walked into the waters of Lake Killarney. He sank into the lake and never was seen alive again.

Each May Day morning for centuries after, however, O'Donoghue visited his earthly home. Just as the sun touched Mount Glenaa near the lake, the waters would begin to churn, and in a shower of glittering spray, O'Donoghue, riding a white charger, would burst through the surface. Trailing behind him were crowds of youths and maidens who danced to the music of silver bells and followed the chieftain across the water, disappearing with him in the mists around the lake.

The time was coming, however, when mortals who crossed the border into Faerie – if they could cross at all – had no choice about returning. They were lost to their own world and their own kind forever, unless another mortal rescued them, which sometimes happened. The borders between the worlds would begin to close, and mortals would no longer be able to touch fairy gold or eat fairy food in safety. They would long for fairy lovers – and sometimes take them – but those loves would be the source of endless sorrow.

It was said, too, that as the centuries passed, the Tuatha and their kind dwindled in size. When they were glimpsed riding in procession or dancing in the night, they were not tall kings and queens, but creatures no bigger than the length of a man's hand – and no louder than a chorus of insects twittering in the grass. The women were perfect in figure and feature, and resplendent in gowns of gauze and gold. As for the tiny knights, they wore cunningly fashioned armor that glittered like faceted gems. The air all around them twinkled with fairy lights, and it was deliciously clean and sweet, charged with a wild scent that lingered long after they disappeared.

It was said that eventually the princes of fairyland became smaller still – so small that they rode saddled grasshoppers instead of horses and sported armor made of fish scales. They lived no longer beneath hill and sea, but in the hollows of oak trees, or in the cowslip's bell or under the leaves of alder and birch.

The heroic fairies thus gradually disappeared as a separate species. They were absorbed into the teeming population of earth fairies that had thronged forest and field and stream and lake ever since the world was shaped.

*From an underwater kingdom unfathomable to man, the Irish
chieftain O'Donoghue — a willing exile from the mortal world — rose with the May Day sun and
galloped across the waters. To see him was an omen of good luck.*

A shimmer on the dark surface of a pond, observed closely, might resolve into an elegant scene

A World in Miniature

For centuries, country folk looked for signs of fairy life in forest and hedgerow on such propitious nights as Midsummer Eve. No more than a trembling leaf or a faint glow near the ground might betray the presence of tiny fairy troops. When a mortal ventured closer, the fairies would vanish, quick to guard their privacy. But a person who approached gently might hear a few notes from miniature flutes and see the sparkle and swirl of revelry for an instant before all went dark.

Diminished descendants of the potent fairies known to mortals at the beginning of time, the trooping fairies of field and forest preserved the courtly habits of their ancestors. In a realm where a leaf was a stately canopy, a thorn a cruel goad and a robin a formidable intruder, they spent their days with music, feasting, sport and war. Although they were comely of feature and resplendent in their garb of petals and thistledown, these jewel-like beings were a race in decline. Mortals who glimpsed their luminous kingdoms sometimes reported seeing fairy funerals, stately and wan – proof, it was said, that while fairies were long-lived, they were not immortal.

ve and courtship, cupped in the petals of a water lily.

In the moonlight of a summer's night, the stems

...wers served as winding staircases and many-colored moths as tiny soaring steeds.

Friend to humankind, and especially to gardeners, the robin was a b

ill omen. But for the fairies, it was said, the creatures provided fine sport.

Walking alone in his garden once, a poet saw a broad leaf move, revealing a tiny procession that bo

...ody on a rose-leaf bier. It was a fairy funeral.

Chapter Two

Guardians of Field and Forest

Even in the days when most of the world was untamed, few regions matched the mystery of the taiga, the forest of pine, birch, spruce and aspen stretching thousands of miles across Russia. Broken only by misty peat bogs where flickering lights danced at night and by a few small villages huddled within wooden palisades, the taiga was a strange and dangerous dominion. Wolf and bear, tiger and leopard, elk and roebuck roamed freely there. And all the animals, it was whispered in the villages, were ruled by forest fairies called *leshiye*, who were curious beings indeed.

Not many mortals glimpsed a *leshy*, and those who did gave conflicting reports about the creature's appearance. The fairy was as changeable as sunlight on a leaf and usually indistinguishable from his surroundings. A *leshy* might be as tall as an ancient tree, green and tangled as the vines that covered it and shaggy as the bark on its trunk. Or he might be as minute as a field mouse, able to pass unseen through the thickest underbrush. He could appear as a whirlwind of blowing leaves and dust. And, if it took his fancy to do so, a *leshy* could assume the shape of an owl or a wolf or a very old man clothed in furs. It was said that the creature's true shape was manlike, with hair and beard as green as ivy and with the long narrow face, coldly gleaming eyes, curling horns and cloven hoofs of a goat.

In truth, the forest fairy was more often heard than seen. He was capable of producing all the sounds that stirred the taiga—the sighing or howling of the wind, the patter of rain, the rustling of leaves, the echoes in spaces among the tree trunks. The few hardy souls who traveled those deep woods—huntsmen, woodcutters and charcoal burners—knew better than to listen to the seemingly innocuous sounds around them as they walked: The mortal who attended the whispers and mumbles of a *leshy* – and none could tell when sounds came from nature and when from the fairy – might be seduced off the narrow track and into real danger.

For the *leshy* was full of mischief and hostile to mortals. Sometimes he curled, like a child in a cradle, in tree branches and amused himself by sighing, moaning or laughing ominously; a *leshy* who did this was called a *zuibotschnik*, from the Russian word for cradle. Sometimes he settled in the abandoned forest huts that were used by itinerants for shelter. Any mortal who entered a hut that a *leshy* had claimed encroached upon elfin territory: The trespasser was doomed to spend the night cowering before the howling and blowing and rattling of an enraged spirit outside the walls.

In the fullness of his powers, the *leshy* was as capricious as a barbarian king and as complex as the forest itself. The springtime woods resounded as he battled other *leshiye* with screeching winds and roiling floodwaters; in the fall, before retreating underground to sleep out the winter, he was again filled with fury, and the forest beasts fled before his wrath.

In the summer, though, his temperament was sportive. By rearranging signposts, by taking the shape of a friendly traveler generous with advice on shortcuts, or simply by calling out in the plaintive tones of a lost child, the *leshy* could lure a wayfarer farther and farther from the path until he found himself in a fetid swamp or at the dizzy edge of a precipice. As likely as not, the *leshy's* gleeful laughter would then ring out from among the forest shadows.

There were darker tales, too, of women who followed a woeful call that led them into birch copses, where they were raped by goatish *leshiye*. Travelers were tickled to death by the fairy, who bedeviled their sides with twigs and teased their faces with forest grasses until they shrieked with laughter and gasped their last. Those who hoped to thrive in the forest were well advised to mollify the fairy lords with offerings: Herdsmen slaughtered cows and left the carcasses for the *leshiye* before driving their cattle to woodland meadows; hunters set out bread and salt – the one symbolizing life, the other, because of its preservative properties, eternity – as hopeful tokens of lasting friendship.

The Russian *leshiye* counted for only a small fraction of the teeming fairy population that haunted the wilds then. As the noble Tuatha Dé Danann retreated into the mists, reappearing only occasionally and in diminished form, the ancient powers of the nature fairies endured.

In that era, when trade was fitful and towns a rarity, most of European civilization consisted of scattered villages girdled by pastures and by fields of oats and millet and barley. The lives of the peasants were ordered by the rhythms of nature – the spring growth, summer ripening and autumn bounty that brought sustenance, and the harsh and hungry days of winter. Their existences were bounded as well by the tracts of forest or heath that encircled each hamlet.

The wind singer

On a remote isle alive with sea winds and sweet melody lived the sylph known as Ariel – spirit and avatar of the air. He slept in the cowslip's bell, rode merrily on the back of a bat and looked down from the curled clouds on the revels of humans below. With his singing (for all his speech was song), he enchanted men and sometimes drove them mad. He knew how to bind and loose the winds, and how to conjure rain or roaring flame. But his spirit partook too much of the air to flourish in the mortals' world, and the time came when he disappeared, passing wholly into the element from which he long ago had come.

Throughout the natural world, mysterious powers were at play. The ordered patchwork of fields and groves was quickened by forces that ripened the grain and protected the harvest – or allowed it to fall victim to blight or thieves or crows. And in the wider wilderness lurked spirit lords like the *leshiye* or the impish Robin Goodfellow of English woods. Individual trees and shrubs had their own inhabitants, and seductive spirits lived in streams and lakes. Even winds and storms reflected the activities of potent fairy folk.

Tied to the daily round of labor in the fields and fearful of what might lurk beyond the borders of their narrow world, countryfolk rarely ventured into the shadowy woodlands or onto the lonely heath. Inevitably, the nature spirits that the peasantry knew best were those living close by.

How fairies first came to reside in land that was tamed by plow, harrow and scythe is a question that village sages do not answer. Perhaps, at some remote date, they migrated from the surrounding forest fastness, spurred by sheer fairy whimsy. Or perhaps they were the spirits of those vanished patches of wasteland or woods that were cleared and put to the plow. Whatever their origin, they had become patrons of grain and fruit over the course of time and were among a toiling peasant's greatest allies. They punished thieves and shirkers and anyone else who stood in the way of a bountiful harvest.

In the wheat fields of Russia, for instance, dwelled a spirit called the *polevik*. Few ever saw him among the dense stalks, for he was extraordinarily nimble and had the ability to vary his height. During the spring, he grew with the stalks of wheat, but after the harvest he shrank to the height of the stubble. Nonetheless, shirkers who napped amid the grain knew him well, for in the afternoons he roamed the fields on a pony that kicked the sleepers and showered them with clods.

In Germany, spirits called *Kornböcke* not only guarded the grain but also caused it to ripen. As elusive as the *polevik*, they rode the breezes that rippled the wheat fields, hid stock-still among the stalks in the guise of blue cornflowers, or prowled the fields as ill-tempered goats.

It is not always clear whether these fairies acted out of concern for the interests of the peasants or simply to protect the fields and groves that were their home. The fairies of English hazel thickets – so familiar that they were known by such homely names as Churn-milk Peg and Melch Dick – were said to inflict painful bloat and cramps on anyone who tore off unripe nuts; they were probably angered more by the damage done to the trees than by the theft. Still, a story of one domesticated orchard elf leaves little doubt that these spirits of nature sometimes developed loyalty toward their weaker mortal neighbors, if those neighbors acted in the fairies' interests.

Among the rolling hills of Dorset, it was said, a wild, frisky colt roamed the apple orchards, never seen by an orchard's rightful owner but instantly and terrifyingly visible to thieves, whom he could paralyze with a glance from his apple green eyes. The story concerns a widow who depend-

England's boisterous mischief-maker

"I am that merry wanderer of the night," cried the elf Robin Goodfellow, sometimes called Puck by countryfolk. Indeed, he was the jester of Faerie, a cutup who lured travelers into swamps, pinched lazy housemaids and pulled stools from beneath inveterate gossips. It was said that humans danced to his seductive piping as trained bears to a circus drum, and that he took his pleasure in causing confusion among mortals, whose various follies he never tired of watching.

ed for her living on two groves of stout trees, the fruit of which fetched a fine price at market. She was old, however, and stiff in the joints – no longer able to keep watch over her apples as in the past. A neighbor, a little skilled in black magic, decided one autumn night to rob her groves.

Thinking to protect himself from the elvish orchard-guardian's gimlet stare, the man climbed into an apple hamper – a large wicker basket – and recited a few spells to send it bounding down the back lanes of the village and into the widow's orchard. The basket settled in the middle of the

grove, and the conjurer murmured another spell. At once, apples flew off the branches and pelted into the hamper. Cursing his bad planning, the thief weathered the stinging hail of apples until one especially firm one smacked him in the eye.

His eye streaming, he leaped out of the hamper – and instantly felt sharp teeth on his rump. Around the hamper of ill-gotten apples the fairy colt chased him, kicking and biting until the thief swerved and fetched up face-to-face with a baleful green stare.

The next morning, the widow entered her grove and found the magician torn and bitten, standing motionless next to his hamper of apples. The fairy colt was nowhere to be seen.

The thief had known well what he risked when he tried to rob that orchard, for the colt's brisk whinny was familiar in the village, and in any case, trees had served as homes and shelters for hosts of the creatures of Faerie since earliest times. The woodlands of ancient Greece, for instance, were haunted by multitudes of nymphs. Some, given to dancing in deserted groves and forests, were known as dryads, from the word *drus*, meaning "tree." Nymphs called hamadryads each were part of a particular tree; the hamadryad's body merged with the bark and leaves, so that if the tree were chopped down, the nymph would perish.

Nymphs and their descendants lingered for centuries in the forests of Europe. In Germany, wood elves sheltered in trees, using the holes in trunks for doorways. And many trees in such northern climes contained fairies of the hamadryad type, whose lives were bound to leaf and bough. The Czechs, for instance, told a tale of a willow fairy who walked by day in the world of mortals, retreating to her graceful tree each night. She married a mortal, bore him a baby and lived happily with him until – all unknowing – he chopped down her tree. The fairy died at once. Her grieving husband made from the willow tree a cradle that had the power to lull the fairy's infant to instant sleep.

No one could say just which of the trees that marked boundaries, overhung village wells or shaded churchyards might be haunted, but it was wise to show particular respect toward any tree that age, disease or storm had twisted or blasted. Such trees were the most likely to harbor spirits.

Certain kinds of trees, too, commonly partook of the supernatural. English oaks found in copses where saplings had grown from the roots of felled trees were homes for oakmen, dwarfish creatures unfriendly to intruders. (The presence of bluebells in these copses was a sign that oakmen were present and that mortals should walk warily.) The elder tree housed a guardian spirit known in England and Denmark by the same name – Elder Mother. She was so protective of her tree's well-being that prudent villagers never failed to ask the fairies' permission before picking elderberries. It was thought best, when clearing a field, to leave the elders standing and plow awkward detours around them. Whoever felled an elder tree risked – at the least – seeing his livestock carried off by sickness. The price could be higher, however. It could be much higher, as a Derbyshire farm family discovered.

Every Midsummer Eve, even in his old age, the father of this family had climbed the hill behind his cottage to lay primroses at the foot of three elders that crowned the hill. On his deathbed, he entreated his three sons to continue this ritual. But two of the sons were made of different stuff and scorned to show respect to trees, fairies or no. Only the youngest continued the custom.

Such devotion rankled the older brothers. Eventually, one of them seized an ax and set off up the hill to put an end to this folly. When he returned, his clothes were flecked with fragrant green wood and his face was ashen. He could not speak of what he had seen or felt as his ax bit into the fairy wood. For days he withered on his pallet; finally he died. By then the second brother had felled another tree, and his end was the same. Only the youngest brother—and a lone tree—remained. And all his life, and during the lives of his children as well, primroses graced the fairy tree each year at Midsummer Eve.

The kinship of such spirit life to the primeval wilderness is clearer in the light of certain tales travelers told of forest trees ensouled by fairies. The trees were similar in character to village trees but immensely more potent, for the ancient powers of Faerie lingered long and strong in places unconquered by humanity. Willows growing in the forest, it was said, sometimes followed wanderers, muttering threats as they creaked and shuffled malevolently along the forest floor. On the moors of Somerset, a female spirit called the One with the White Hand flickered from birch copses, as pale and gaunt as the trees, to ambush young travelers. If she brushed a youth's head with her spidery hand, he would go mad. If she touched his breast, he would fall dead.

Such were the risks of wandering far from the relative security of the villages. Even the ordinary rigors of travel were daunting in those days: A journey to another village could take many hours or several days under the best conditions—and travelers rarely met the best conditions. Most often, they encountered mud, swollen streams and matted undergrowth.

Even when the path was open and the season favorable, misfortune could strike. Waiting in vain for an overdue wayfarer, fellow villagers could only speculate: He might have blundered into a quagmire, tumbled into a forest pool or followed a vision of sylvan loveliness until his mortal ties seemed mere wisps.

The spirits at bay beyond the fringe of fields could bring about all these things and more. But their favorite way to display power to mortal intruders was to mislead them. Among different spirits there were, to be sure, differences of style. While the *leshiye* used mimicry to confuse wanderers, the *gwyllion* had another tactic. These fairies roamed the mountains of Wales, caring for goats, whose beards they combed each Wednesday, the day said to be the fairies' Sunday. They sometimes took the form of goats themselves but more generally appeared as old women, and they disliked mortals.

A Welshman—"of undoubted veracity," in his neighbors' estimation—was toiling

up a mountainside one night when he discerned in the gloom the bent figure of a crone, her ash-colored garments barely distinguishable from the bracken. She trudged slowly along the stony path, and it seemed a simple matter to catch up with her. But though he quickened his steps, he drew no closer, and although he hailed her, she would not turn around. Puzzled and annoyed, he hurried toward the ever-receding figure. He soon forgot himself and the purpose of his journey and everything else except the drab figure ahead. Only when the ground beneath his feet grew soggy did he stop, realizing that in his single-minded pursuit he had strayed far from his path and blundered into a swamp. Just then, a crackle of ancient laughter rang out through the marshland vapors, and the man knew that a *gwyllion* had tricked him. Remembering that fairies often feared iron, he drew his knife, and the laughter stopped. He was alone and hopelessly lost in the dark, and there was nothing for it but to wait out the night in that forsaken swamp. That story recurs with countless variations in travelers' tales from those days. It is often difficult to tell whether the spirits of forest and mountain spun their deceptions in order to discourage mortal trespassing or simply to amuse themselves. But their playful natures always clouded when mortals despoiled their domain. Even at that early date, when game was plentiful, mortal lords laid

claim to hunting preserves. Every beast within the boundaries of such a preserve was reserved for the lord's pleasure. Peasants who filched a hare from the meadows or a fat pike from the streams risked punishment. The same held true in the wider wilderness ruled by fairies: Its stags, boars, bears, and even the tiniest of its furred and feathered denizens, were the jealously guarded property of a fairy master, to dispose of as he pleased. In Russia once, travelers reported a mysterious migration of squirrels that turned the forest floor into a squirming, leaping carpet of fur. According to those who knew the forest, the explanation was simple: *Leshiye* were notorious gamblers; one had had a run of bad luck and was paying off a neighboring *leshy* with his entire constituency of squirrels.

Possession bred possessiveness, as is shown in a Scottish tale of two lads who went hunting and received a lesson in the proprieties of the wilderness. It was a chill morning, with an icy blue sky and a wind sweet with heather. The lads were townsfolk, in search of sport and relief from the cramped alleys of their village. As they pushed through the gorse and heather, hares sprang from hiding and pheasants struggled into the air. The youths loosed arrow after arrow. Most missed the mark, but in the end their hours on the moor yielded a brace of fowl and three hares — a fine day's hunting.

Weary from the chase, the lads took their ease in a grassy glen by a stream. As one of the hunters rested his head on a tussock and stared at the sky, the other bent to drink the water. A shadow dimmed the sparkle of the stream, and when he raised his eyes, he met the furious gaze of the Brown Man of the Moors.

There was no mistaking him, for every Scottish lad was weaned on tales of the master of the moors, of his fearsome aspect and frightful temper. His build was squat, but his thick limbs and knobby hands conveyed an impression of elemen-

Haven for a host of spirits

When magic pervaded the woodlands of Europe, no tree was more revered than the mighty oak — the Monarch of the Forest, as a chronicler called it. In the rustling of its leaves could be heard the voice of a hamadryad, that tree's own spirit, whose face peered from the wrinkled bark as if through a murky glass. And other spirits — given different names in different countries — lived in the branches, leaves and roots of the oak.

Most easily visible of the arboreal band were the tree elves — gnarled little men and graceful women who might be spied dancing along the branches to the music of crickets and frogs in the shifting, speckled light of a summer's day. More difficult to detect were the Moss Maidens of Germany —

beneficent fairies wise in the healing properties of plants – who camouflaged their old, furrowed faces and bodies in moss that they wove to dress the roots of a tree.

Within the root systems of German trees lived tiny *Kobolds* – malignant sprites given to plaguing homeowners unless wooed with bribes of food. In Italy, *salvanelli* occupied cavities in the oak; these playful imps dressed in worn red overalls or jerkins and were much addicted to stealing the milk of farmers and riding their horses to exhaustion.

In Sweden, the great horned owls that wheeled through the forest twilight and settled on the branches of oak trees were said to be the dangerous, shape-shifting wood elves known as *skogsra*. And the British said that the wild flowers – cowslips, wild thyme, foxglove and bluebells – found at the foot of the oak each enfolded a pillywiggin, a diminutive fairy that dwelled where only a bee can fly.

tal strength. His head sprouted a mass of tangled red curls, his garments were the brown of withered bracken, and his broad feet were bare and callused. He gripped a stout staff and ground it into the earth as he vented his fury.

Ke berated the youths for trespassing on his moors and cursed them for slaying the beasts that were his subjects. For him, he declared, the apples, nuts and whortleberries he gathered were meat enough. The moors had secrets that only he could reveal, said the Brown Man, and his voice grew honeyed. He could teach them much, if only they would follow him to his lair. The first lad stepped forward to accept the Brown Man's invitation, but his companion caught his sleeve. "He will tear you to pieces if you cross the brook," said the youth, knowing that only the barrier of running water – always a hedge against fairies bent on evil – kept the Brown Man from attacking them. When his invitation was spurned, the sprite danced with rage; then he vanished, leaving only a patch of disturbed ground.

Although the first lad had escaped for the moment, his impulsive nature was his undoing in the end. On the trek back, he thoughtlessly shot a final hare. Before the year was out, he sickened and died, and no one doubted that the Brown Man of the Moors had wasted his strapping frame.

In spite of such hazards, humankind could not turn away from the wilderness altogether. Its game, berries and mushrooms were welcome additions to villagers' dull daily fare, and it yielded wood to heat peasants' cottages and to fire village smithies. In the summer herdsmen drove their cattle into the forest to forage for sweet grasses, and in the autumn swineherds followed with their pigs, to fatten them on acorns. And there was the sheer extent of the wilderness, the fact that any interchange between neighboring settlements – and the human appetite for news was sharp – had to be conducted through a barrier of forest.

Offerings of food and drink went far toward mollifying the patron spirits of the wild, as did a respectful demeanor. When passing through a *leshy's* domain, for instance, a wanderer was well advised not to whistle or shout. And one sure way to anger the diminutive Moss Maidens – busy spinners who made the moss for German forests – was to mutilate a sapling.

The mortals who fared best in the wilderness – and sometimes were unexpectedly blessed by the fairies' good will – were those of humble and guileless heart, folk who entered the spirits' territory well aware that they were there on sufferance. Such a one was a woodcutter who, journeying through the mountains of Bohemia on a summer's day so hot that the high cliffs shimmered with heat, came upon a cobalt blue forest pool. It seemed bottomless, and the breezes that stirred it carried away a chill.

The woodsman shivered in the stillness. It came to him that this was no ordinary pond but a secret retreat of Rübezahl, a spirit of those forest-clad mountains. Few accounts of Rübezahl agree on his appearance, and in fact he seems to have taken a dazzling variety of guises. Some chron-

In any of a dozen guises, the mountain spirit called Rübezahl wandered German forests with staff in hand—overseeing his dominions, summoning snow or sunshine, and meting out rough magic to mortals who crossed his path.

iclers claim that his true shape was that of a brawny elf, as rugged as the granite mountains he haunted, but travelers reported meeting him in the outward forms of all of the solitary mortals commonly encountered in the mountains: wandering monks, charcoal burners, herb gatherers, hunters, woodsmen and guides. Winning the confidence of other wayfarers, Rübezahl gleefully misled them. He was also known to perform a conjurer's range of tricks, confounding travelers with phantasms and freak storms.

At this forest pool on this afternoon, however, no one was in sight, no storms threatened and no illusions flickered behind the curtain of pines. But before the man knelt at the water's edge to drink, he loudly begged Rübezahl's pardon, explaining that he was very thirsty. And after he had drunk and filled his water flask, he again addressed Rübezahl and thanked him heartily. Then he went on his way.

Presently the sun and the dusty track again made him thirsty, and he unhooked the flask from his belt, uncorked it and put it to his lips. Although it felt full and heavy – strangely heavy, in fact – not a drop of water or even a breath of moisture met his parched tongue. Frustrated, the woodsman smashed the flask on a stone. Then his eyes widened, for amid the splintered crockery glittered chunks of precious topaz, some of them veined with gold. Rübezahl had heard his courteous words and rewarded him.

The occasional beneficence of the fairy masters of forest and mountain did not blind countryfolk to the rift between the changeable realm of nature spirits and the steadier world of humankind. Faerie, with its curious inhabitants, was ultimately unattainable for mortals – but for that very reason it had a powerful allure. The most fearful quality of many nature fairies, in fact, was their fatal attractiveness.

The danger was trivial in the case of roughhewn, earthy spirits such as the Brown Man and Rübezahl, whose powers, though considerable, did not include seduction. But the risk of enchantment was strong for young men venturing into the mountains of Scandinavia, for there they might meet the *huldra*, a beguiling, white-robed forest nymph whose beauty was marred only by her tail, tasseled like that of a cow, and her back, which was as hollow as a cheese mold.

A youth who allowed the *huldra* to lure him to her mountain fastness as her paramour might one day return to human society. But the lover of a *huldra* was altered forever, in body or in mind. The stigma might be no more than a beardless chin, where the *huldra* had licked him in a fit of passion; or he might be touched with madness. The effect was the same: to set him apart permanently from the world of mortals, to isolate him from his own kind.

No less perilous to susceptible young men were the golden-haired *vile* of Central Europe. These mistresses of the forest spoke the language of animals, tended herds of chamois and deer – and were enchantingly beautiful. Their bodies were as slim and pliant as the stems of young pines, their eyes flashed like a dapple of forest sunshine, and their songs rose in a golden thread of melody above the rustle of foliage. A man who glimpsed a *vila*

A savage and treacherous water spirit hungry for children's blood, the kelpie haunted Scottish rivers and lochs in the shape of a wild gray horse.

was doomed. He would yearn for her so desperately that he would become a stranger to all who knew him, and in the end he would die.

The most dangerous among the nature fairies were the spirits of streams, ponds and lakes. The *vodianoy* of Russia, green-haired and as bloated as drowned men, lived near water mills and afflicted nocturnal intruders with water sickness—dropsy—so that their bodies filled like sponges with liquid. The Scandinavian *neck* sometimes sat serenely on the glassy surface of a lake or river, a red cap covering his sunny

The chill clasp of a sylvan spring

What mortal could gaze unscathed into the wild eyes of a water nymph? In Greece lived one who could not – Hylas, an adventurer and a voyager who sailed the blue Aegean Sea. One day, he put ashore at the island of Chios and, leaving his companions, went in search of fresh water. Deep in the forest he came upon a woodland spring where nymphs played among the rushes and water lilies. They beckoned when they saw the beautiful young man, and he approached, kneeling at the spring's edge to fill his pitcher. One of the maidens fixed him with eyes so ardent that Hylas paused, unable to move or look away. Upon his arm he felt hands that were soft but strong, and deathly cold. Before he could speak or cry out, he was pulled from the bank into the weed-choked depths of the spring.

Hylas never was seen again. His companions searched the island for days, shouting his name in every grove and grotto. At last, they came to the spring, and there they were answered: As though from a great distance, Hylas called out, reaching hopelessly toward them from a watery world that he would never escape.

ringlets, and played a golden harp. He required a human sacrifice each year, and his shriek of "Cross over!" echoed eerily on riverbanks following any drowning.

In the mournful northern waters of Scotland lived the malign kelpie, who sometimes took the form of a handsome gray horse that could be seen galloping along the stony banks of a loch. All such horses were not suspect, of course; a crofter, watching from a nearby hill, would breathe easier if he saw a lone gray horse trot up to a groom he knew or docilely submit to a rider. But if the beast veered out into the lake, its hoofs striking foam across the choppy surface of the water and clearing the ripples as if they were solid ground, the watcher would hurry off to warn his family that the feared water horse was abroad.

Like many other water spirits, the kelpie was fatally charming, and children often succumbed to his wiles. When, with eyes flashing and velvety coat rippling, he cantered up to a group of children playing at the water's edge, they rarely could resist stroking his neck and mounting his back. Once astride him, there was no escape, for their limbs stuck fast to the kelpie's flanks. With his terrified cargo, the kelpie galloped out into deep water, pawed aside the waves and slipped from sight. Somewhere in the depths, it was said, he shook the children from his back and devoured them, leaving only their entrails to wash up on shore.

Water fairies could exert their seductive appeal in many ways. A Norwegian waterfall spirit called the *fossegrim* — golden-haired, fine-featured and no more than a foot high — sang so sweetly that the very trees danced and children hid on riverbanks to hear his charming melodies. Other fairies had the irresistible and perfectly elusive beauty of moving water, as the following story shows:

Every market day in Magdeburg, a north German settlement on the Elbe River, a strange and lovely maiden could be seen among the roistering crowds. Her expression was sweet and serene as she glided among the vendors, glancing at the mounds of cabbages and potatoes, the plump caged fowl and rabbits, and the heaps of crockery and ironware. Her clothes were as sober as those of any merchant's wife, and her expression as detached and judging, but her propriety was belied by her hair, which shimmered like sunshine on water, and her eyes, which were a deep and fascinating green.

For those reasons, and because townsfolk who pressed close to her in the crowd reported that water trickled unceasingly from one corner of her white apron, people said she was a nix — a water maiden, come in search not of goods but of suitable young men — and mothers warned their sons to keep clear of her.

The advice, however, was not always heeded. One afternoon, as the chattering vendors packed up their wares and the crowd thinned, a fisherman followed the nix through the narrow streets of Magdeburg and out into the forest. Her golden hair glittered far ahead, and he fixed his eye on it as he trailed her through the pines to the riverbank, far above the town. There she turned and, smiling radiantly, invited the fisherman to join her and her people in their watery realm. Then she stepped into the river and vanished into the swift, dark current.

The fisherman lacked the courage to follow the nix that day. But by the next market day, his longing had grown so sharp that he was deaf to his friends' pleadings, and even though they pursued him and continued to call out warnings, he followed the fairy down the steep bank and into the river. He stood poised on the water's surface for an instant, then sank. On the bank his friends watched and waited. Suddenly a fountain of blood,

black in the fading light of late afternoon, erupted from the very spot where he had vanished. A moment later, it subsided. The horrified observers knew that they would never see their companion again.

Overarching the spirit-charged expanses of field, forest and heath, and the fairy mansions of trees, streams, lakes and waterfalls, was a realm even more mysterious in its workings and more capricious in its effects—the sky. Here, too, spirits dwelled. Storms and the change of seasons were their work.

They were not unique in having control over weather. The *leshiye*, Rübezahl and other forest spirits were known to conjure up storms; this action was local, however—often no more than a theatrical display intended to confound a traveler or woodsman. The spirits who colored and then withered leaves with autumn chill, heaped up shoals of snow across the winter landscape and ushered in spring were a more remote lot, grandly aloof from the mortals to whom their doings could mean life or death.

Accounts of these spirits of weather and season rarely convey any sense of their character—only of their power. But a Russian tale of Frost, who roamed the winter woods, leaping from tree to tree and snapping his fingers, gives a glimpse of that spirit's capacity for kindness.

Once, a simple and virtuous girl lived in a cottage with her two stepsisters, her cruel stepmother and her loving but ineffectual father. In the dead of winter, the stepmother, thinking to rid herself of the girl,

Storm-borne Queen from a realm of ice

Beautiful as an ice crystal, the fairy called the Snow Queen was much loved by Danish children but dangerous to those whose love she returned. An old tale tells how this was so.

Once, on a cold winter's day in a northern city, a small boy sat in his little attic room watching the snowflakes blow against the windowpane. A particularly large and lacy flake stuck to the glass and caught his eye. It glittered and spread across the pane until it took the shape of a tall woman hovering in the winter air. Smiling radiantly, she beckoned to the boy through the glass, then disappeared. Entranced, he ran down the stairs and out into the street. There he found the Snow Queen – for it was she – awaiting him in a white sledge drawn by white horses. She gave him her hand, and he climbed into the sledge among the snowy furs that filled it. At once the sledge began to move, tearing through the winter streets and climbing into the air.

Over ditches and hedgerows they flew, with the snow driving in their faces. As they soared, the Queen put her icy lips to the little boy's forehead, and he felt a chill that pierced to his heart. But the fairy only smiled and urged the horses on. At last the wild ride ended at the fairy's winter palace, set on a plain of ice in Lapland.

The boy might have remained forever as the shivering inmate of the Snow Queen's palace. But in Denmark he had a friend who loved him dearly, a little girl who all alone searched the wide world until she found him. Her adventures are the stuff of another tale. What matters is that, invincible in her fidelity, she rescued her companion and returned him to the gentling sun. As for the Snow Queen, alone in her wind-swept, frozen halls, she wept icy tears and waited for the chance to find another child.

ordered the man to take his daughter into the woods as a bride for Frost.

The girl was a trusting soul. Believing that her stepmother had found her a proper husband, she rose joyfully the next morning, dressed in her best clothes and, clutching the few small items that formed her trousseau, climbed into a sledge. But when her grief-stricken father drove her deep into the forest, she knew that she was destined for no mortal bridegroom.

They drew up under a tall pine. The father helped the girl out of the sledge. "Sit here and await the bridegroom," said the old man wretchedly. "And receive him as pleasantly as you can."

So the girl was left alone, already pierced with cold. There was no chance of escape from the deep snow and stinging wind, and soon her cries sounded as no more than a rattle of teeth. Then from among the whitened trees came the sound of Frost. He was leaping briskly from pine to pine, cracking the branches, snapping his fingers and cackling to himself. The next moment he was in the tree above her.

He demanded: "Are you warm, maid?"

"Yes, I'm warm, warm, dear Father Frost," she answered. Frost, after all, was a powerful elf, to be treated with respect. She clasped her arms across her freezing breast.

But Frost only leaned down from the tree, closer to her. His breath was icicles. She could scarcely speak when he asked his question again, but she managed to whisper, "Warm am I, Frost dear, yes, warm, Father dear!"

By this time Frost was touching her. She could feel his fingers dancing over her body, encircling her throat, reaching for her heart. She felt her life slipping away when he asked for the third time: "Are you warm, pretty one?"

With no more than a sigh, she replied that she was.

Then Frost's ice heart melted, and instead of his deathly cold grasp the girl suddenly felt his presence warm and gentle about her. He tenderly wrapped her in furs and blankets and held her until she closed her eyes. The night passed thus, and when her father returned the next day, prepared to mourn her, he found her sleeping under a warm cloak of fur. Beside her was a rich bridal veil and a pannier of gifts. He stooped to wake her where she lay in the snow, scarcely believing his eyes. But his daughter rose cheerfully and stepped into the sledge beside him for the drive home.

Their reception at their cottage was as might have been expected. At first the stepmother was furious, but as she inspected the furs and gifts she grew silent. "If Frost is so generous to this homely girl," she thought, "what will he not give to my own two handsome daughters?" So the next morning she ordered them into the sledge, and the father drove the spoiled pair into the forest.

During the sledge ride the daughters quarreled about which one of them the splendid bridegroom would favor. But when they were seated beneath the pine tree and Frost bore down on them, cracking and snapping in a blast of cold, they began to complain.

"Are you warm, maidens?" demanded Frost. "Are you warm, pretty ones?"

They knew no courtesy. "Get along

with you!" they cried. "Our hands and feet are quite dead."

Frost drew closer still, and ice crystals sparkled in the air as he sought their answer once again. But the chill nipped their limbs, and they cried, "Let us be! Out of sight, cursed breath of winter!"

Frost showed no mercy. When the man arrived the next morning, his stepdaughters were frozen as stiff as boards.

Not often did the controllers of sky and weather show any concern for mortals. More typical of the forbidding aspect of these spirits was the Blue Hag— known in Gaelic as the Cailleac Bheur, or Old Wife—who brought winter to the Scottish Highlands. At the beginning of time, when the worlds of mortals and spirits had not yet grown asunder, she was a familiar sight on the wind-swept hills. Her face, the legends say, was blue with cold, her hair as white as a frosted aspen and the plaid that wrapped her meager shoulders was the dun of wintry stubble. Each year, after Allhallows, she strode the moors and summits, smiting the earth with her heavy staff to beat down the grasses and harden the earth with frost.

In winter, reveling in her victory over the forces of growth, she unleashed tempests and blizzards. But in the spring, her power waned as sap rose in the vegetation. Day by day she weakened as the earth quickened anew, and on the Eve of May Day she gave up the struggle: In a final fury she flung her staff under a holly tree—where to this day no grass can grow—and stiffened and shrank into a soli-

tary gray stone, to wait out the summer.

After those earliest days, as villages began to dot the wilds, meetings with the Cailleac grew rare. As human beings domesticated their world with hedges and boundary markers and neat furrows, and turned their gaze away from wilderness and sky to the petty cares of the everyday, the Cailleac was seen only in her effects: in ground that one day was soft and fertile, the next iron-hard with frost, in landscapes transformed by the first snowfall of winter. These were evidence enough of the Cailleac's undiminished power.

Later still, when the country villages had swelled into towns, the muddy forest byways had widened into thoroughfares, and here and there in erstwhile forest or field had risen a shrieking forge or a clanging factory, the sky remained as wild as ever, and the seasons rolled on ceaselessly. By all appearances, the Cailleac and her weatherworking kin continued their rounds, pervasive but unseen. But they were exceptions: The natural world was shrinking, and with its decline, the powers of its spirit denizens faded.

As the curtain of forest was rolled back and towns bustled where once fields had spread, the *leshiye*, Rübezahl and all the other spirits of nature shrank from the clamor of burgeoning humanity. They retreated into the remaining tatters of wilderness, shed their expansive ways and became as elusive as shadows. But to this day, a wanderer who tarries in the secret places of a woodland may fleetingly sense the unabated spirit life all around and know that enchantment has not vanished from the world.

Blown by her winter winds from mountain to mountain and followed by the herons that were her special charge, the Cailleac Bheur of Scotland left withered crops and frozen ground where she struck with her death-dealing staff.

The Myrtle Tree's Sweet Tenant

When fairies still whispered among tree branches, the myrtle thrived in Mediterranean lands, and it was home to a generously loving kind of fay. Perhaps this was because the tree had once been sacred to the goddess of love: Venus, an early author wrote, could always be found "sitting under a myrtle shade." Of one of the myrtle fairies, a tale was told in Italy:

A Prince once found delight in the glossy leaves and spicy scent of a certain myrtle tree, which he had placed in its pot on the balcony outside his bedchamber. That very same night— and for six nights more—the Prince heard a patter of feet and felt in the dark a caress as soft as eiderdown; then a fragrant creature slipped under the bedclothes. She sported tenderly with him all through the night.

She always disappeared, however, at the first glimmer of dawn, and the Prince was never able to see her. At last, so that he might capture her as she sought to leave in the early-morning hours, he twisted a tress of her hair around his wrist and summoned his chamberlain for light. The glow of the chamberlain's candle revealed the slender cap-

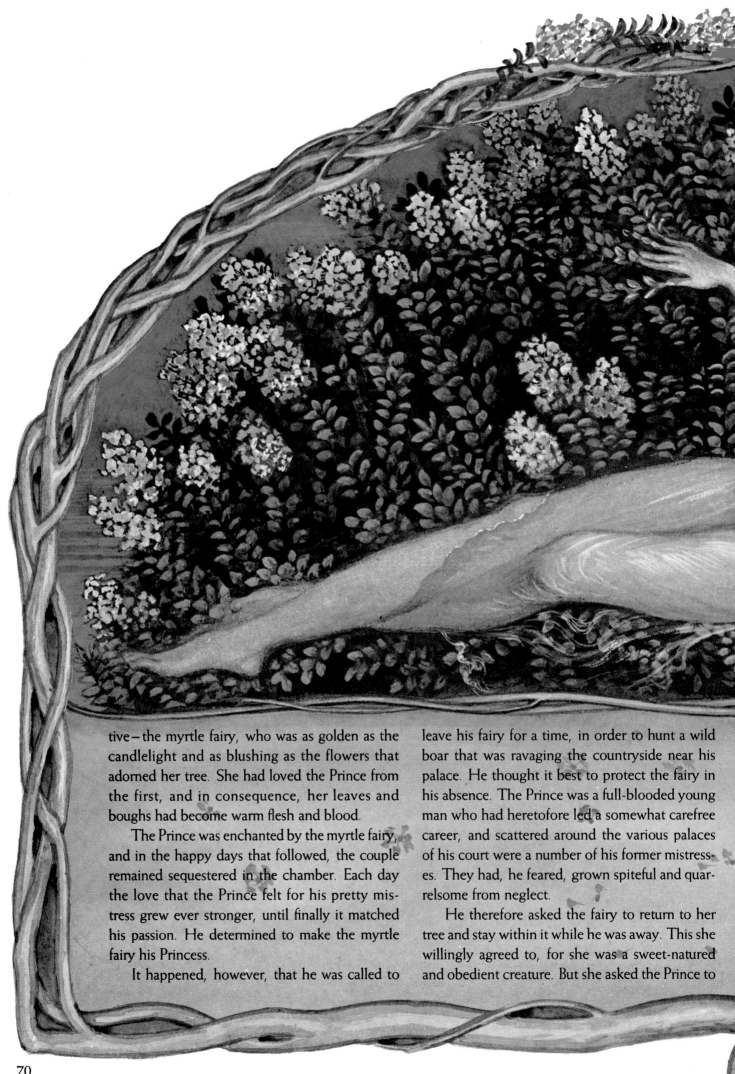

tive—the myrtle fairy, who was as golden as the candlelight and as blushing as the flowers that adorned her tree. She had loved the Prince from the first, and in consequence, her leaves and boughs had become warm flesh and blood.

The Prince was enchanted by the myrtle fairy, and in the happy days that followed, the couple remained sequestered in the chamber. Each day the love that the Prince felt for his pretty mistress grew ever stronger, until finally it matched his passion. He determined to make the myrtle fairy his Princess.

It happened, however, that he was called to leave his fairy for a time, in order to hunt a wild boar that was ravaging the countryside near his palace. He thought it best to protect the fairy in his absence. The Prince was a full-blooded young man who had heretofore led a somewhat carefree career, and scattered around the various palaces of his court were a number of his former mistresses. They had, he feared, grown spiteful and quarrelsome from neglect.

He therefore asked the fairy to return to her tree and stay within it while he was away. This she willingly agreed to, for she was a sweet-natured and obedient creature. But she asked the Prince to

tie a golden bell to one of her branches, so that when he returned from the hunt, he would be able to release her: He had only to pull a silken ribbon that bound the bell to the tree, and the bell's ringing would summon her into his arms.

And then, with a sigh, the fairy slipped into her tree. One moment she stood before the Prince, and the next she was gone and all he could see was a slight trembling of the shining myrtle leaves. He tied the bell to a branch and left, giving instructions to his chamberlain to attend the graceful tree faithfully.

Days passed while the Prince hunted in the countryside. The lovers' bedchamber was silent and empty, save for the wind that ruffled the bed hangings and rustled the leaves of the myrtle tree, safe in its pot on the balcony. In the afternoons the chamberlain watered the tree, but otherwise the fairy was undisturbed.

One morning, however, the door opened and seven whispering women stole into the room. They were the Prince's mistresses, come in search of the new rival, whom none of them had seen. They searched the room thoroughly but found nothing. Eventually they wandered to the balcony to consider the matter.

As the women talked, first one and then another of them began idly to strip the glossy leaves of the myrtle tree. In doing so, one of them pulled the ribbon that rang the golden bell. The bark of the tree trembled, and down stepped the fairy, sunnily smiling.

At once the jealous women sprang upon her. Knives flashed and blood spurted and before many moments had passed, there was nothing left of the myrtle-tree fairy but scattered bits of bone, tattered green leaves and slivers of bark. Only the youngest of the seven mistresses restrained herself: She took no more than a lock of the myrtle fairy's golden hair.

The women then quietly slipped away to their separate chambers, and no one in the palace

was any the wiser about what they had done in those few moments.

In the afternoon, the Prince's chamberlain came to tend the myrtle tree. When he entered the room he halted at once, appalled by the signs of carnage. He considered the matter for some minutes. Finally the chamberlain gathered the bones and leaves and bark together with trembling hands and tucked them into the pot on the balcony. Then he fled, dreading the wrath of the Prince and fearing that he would be held responsible.

The next day, the Prince returned to his chamber, fresh from the outdoors and eager for his fairy mistress. But what sight welcomed him? On the balcony stood the myrtle tree's pot, with nothing more in it than white shards of bone and the

broken twigs and brown leaves
of the fairy's tree. He called, but no
voice answered. His heart turned to ice.
He began to weep.

For weeks the Prince kept to his bedchamber, mourning alone. But as he
mourned, a curious thing was happening on the
balcony outside the chamber. The torn scraps of
myrtle leaves and bark were washed with soft rains
and warmed by the sun, and as the days passed the
plant began to grow. First, pale green shoots appeared, then slender branches, then larger ones.
One morning, the myrtle tree sprang at last into
full-blown flower, and from it stepped the fairy,
whole again and golden as sunshine.

When the kissing ceased, the myrtle-tree fairy
told the Prince what had happened. He decided
that he would marry his mistress at once, and he
pondered the ways he could avenge the injury.
And this is what he did:

The wedding was celebrated in the palace with
a magnificent banquet, to which the entire court
was invited. After the feasting, the Prince posed a
question: What should be the punishment, he demanded, of the man or woman who would injure
his Princess? The gallows, said one courtier. The
wheel, said another.

When it came the turn of the mistresses, they
were of one accord: Such a person, they said,
should be thrown into a dungeon and left to lan-
guish until death.

"As you have decreed," said the Prince, "so it
shall be done." And he ordered the women imprisoned, sparing only the youngest, who had taken
but a lock of the fairy's hair.

Chapter Three

Of Fairy Raids and Mortal Missteps

Before the time of towns and highways, in the days when the stone strongholds of Irish chieftains towered beside the fairy hills of the Tuatha Dé Danann, a mortal woman was stolen from her kinsfolk and taken to live in the underground palace of an elfin King. This is what happened:

The woman, whose name was Ethna, was the flower of Ireland. She was lily fair, with hair of red-gold, and she was the bride of a young lord of Connacht. His delight in her was such that he celebrated the marriage with weeks of merrymaking. By day, hunting parties coursed the woods and meadows beyond his castle walls; by night, the torches blazed high, the goblets brimmed with bright wine and harpers played leaping melodies for the dances of the court. In the center of the dancers whirled Ethna the bride, surrounded by the clouds of silk that made her wedding dress. Each evening she danced thus, until one midnight her hand slipped suddenly from her partner's and she crum-

pled to the flagstones. The harps fell silent and the courtiers drew back to let the young lord kneel beside his bride. He spoke her name, but never a word did Ethna reply. Her rosy blush had died, her breath was as shallow as a kitten's and her eyes were closed. She was borne to her chamber, and all through the night her husband watched at her bedside.

When the morning sun slanted across her counterpane, Ethna opened heavy-lidded eyes and spoke, but her husband understood little of what she said, and that little did not still his unease. In a faraway, toneless voice, Ethna told him that while she slept she had dreamed of the palace of a mighty King. The sun never shone in that place, she said, but the halls gleamed with their own radiance, and the music that drifted through them vanquished every mortal care. All that Ethna now desired was to sleep and to dream of that world once more.

And sleep she did, all through that day, pale and still as a figure carved on a tomb. No one could wake her. When the shadows lengthened into night, her childhood nurse was sent to watch over her so that her husband could rest. The old woman nodded and dozed and woke shivering in the small hours. The chamber was cool and still. A moment later, the woman's wail echoed down the palace corridors. Ethna's bed lay white and empty in the moonlight. Only the dimpled sheets showed where she had rested.

The remainder of that long night was spent in anxious and angry conference, and at the first gleam of dawn, the young bridegroom rode out with a company of his retainers, setting a fast pace for the hill called Knockma. The grassy swell of that hill concealed the underground palaces of Finvarra, King of the Tuatha in Connacht and long a friend and adviser of the young lord; if anyone could find the missing bride, it surely would be he.

The green surface of the mound at Knockma gave no hint of the underground splendor in which the King dwelled. But as the riders emerged from the woodland fringing the rise, a busy twittering filled the air, as if a flock of finches had settled in the trees. The riders paused and listened, and at last a single voice grew intelligible. The lord began to understand the words, and his features became grim. Finvarra had betrayed his trust: The twitter was the sound of fairy voices in the air, and its subject was the King's great joy in his new mistress, the Lily of Ireland, whom Finvarra had seduced from her kinsfolk and taken in thrall.

The lord barked orders, and messengers wheeled their horses and galloped off, eager to do his bidding. Before long a column of peasants, carrying scythes and spades on their shoulders, emerged from the woods and fell to the task their lord had set: to dig down to the Fairy King's hidden realm and rescue the captive mortal bride. All through that day, while the husband watched from his saddle, the peasants worked, and by nightfall, a great dark cleft gaped on one flank of the grassy rise. The laborers rested, well satisfied.

In the morning, however, the work camp awakened to discover a discouraging sight: The pit they had dug had vanished, and the knoll's mantle of turf spread unbroken over the site of yesterday's toil. Invisible and silent, Finvarra had exercised his powers. For three days the peasants labored in vain as, night after night, Finvarra confounded their efforts. The workers grumbled among themselves, and the young lord grieved.

Then disembodied voices fluted above the mound once more, and the husband heard them. "If salt is spread on the broken earth, the mortals' work will be safe," said a whisper on the wind.

Salt was known for its power over fairies. The lord dispatched riders to every corner of Connacht to buy salt at any price—for salt was a rare commodity in those days. And after another day's digging, and a night's waiting, the salt proved its worth: The excavations of the day before were untouched. The white layer of salt crystals that covered the broken earth was undisturbed.

now the laborers worked willingly, and by afternoon a deep glen gashed the fairy hill. Those who dug could hear movement and voices behind the wall of earth, and the voices were no longer musical and gay but shrill and fearful. If the light of day shone upon fairy halls, the voices said, those halls would crumble. At last a single voice rang out through the earthen barrier, clear and commanding: "Stop your work at once, mortal men. Lay down your spades, and at sunset the bride will be given back to her husband."

The Fairy King had spoken. The men left their work, and at sunset the lord waited alone at the head of the glen, his face turned toward his own woodlands. He heard a gentle footfall, turned and beheld his Ethna, solemn and lovely, clad in the same gossamer in which she had been taken prisoner. But the girdle around her waist, intricately embroidered and elaborately knotted, was new.

The lord had little joy in his triumph, for Ethna's spirit remained distant. As the weeks merged into months and winter silvered the land, Ethna sat listless and waxen in her chamber or drifted wraithlike through the echoing corridors. She did not speak, nor did she seem to hear the words of those she had once known and loved. The courtiers whispered among themselves, saying with sadness that the bride had eaten fairy food and thus had lost her soul. The young lord brooded over his puppet wife, and he kept apart from the others.

A full year after Ethna's return, the lord was out riding alone when he heard the fairy voices one last time. Again, a faint fluting in the air swelled and resolved itself into a conversation. One voice said that Ethna's spirit dwelled still with the fairies. A second voice replied that what bound her was the embroidered girdle. If the husband took the girdle from Ethna's waist

An amorous abductress

Famed among fairies was Morgan le Fay, beautiful, wise and passionately fond of mortal men. Many tales surround her name, but most agree that Morgan ruled an enchanted island of apples – Avalon – and most say that she took King Arthur of Britain there when defeat overcame him. She took another brave knight to live with her in Avalon, too. It happened this way:

Once, a fine son was born to the King of Denmark. Six fairies – sisters all – attended the christening, and one of these was Morgan. Each gave a gift to the boy. The first wished him bravery; the second, the chance to display his valor; the third, invincibility; the fourth, the art of pleasing; and the fifth, a loving nature. Morgan, the last and youngest fairy, was enamored of the mortal child. Her gift, therefore, was herself. She said that when the time came, he would join her on her island, there to live as her paramour.

The boy grew into manhood and became a knight of France; he was known, because of his birthplace, as Ogier the Dane. He had a long life, distinguished by valor and adventure, and at last he grew old. Morgan waited no longer. She caused a ship on which he sailed to be wrecked near Avalon. Ogier survived and reached the island, where he found an orchard. Within it was Morgan, as beautiful as the dawn. She slipped a ring on the knight's finger, and the years fell from him: The bent back straightened and the old eyes cleared and he became the youth the fairy desired. With a satisfied smile she placed a crown on his head. Every memory of his mortal life fled.

Thus Ogier the Dane became a willing prisoner of the fairy's love. He lived in Avalon for centuries, the legends say. And for all that mortals know, he may live there still, caught in the timeless thrall of Faerie.

Rough justice for a thieving intruder

When folk in the West Country of England talked of encounters with the fairies, they liked to recall the adventure of a certain old miser who loved gold better than the drunkard his wine or the libertine his women.

Like everybody else in the Cornish town of St. Just, the miser knew that the fairies of the region possessed riches beyond imagining and that these could be seen when the fairies held their midnight revels by the light of the harvest moon. It was worth a man's life to set foot on the hill where the revels were said to be held – "But," thought the miser, "it can do no harm to watch from afar." Accordingly, at the next harvest moon he left the village, alone and on foot, and crept to the fairy hill. There he hid and waited.

The night was so clear that the old man could see each bristle of the

and burned it, and if he removed the pin that adorned the girdle and buried it, the mortal bride would rejoin her kind.

The lord lost no time in returning to Ethna's chamber. He knelt at her side and plucked at her girdle with nervous fingers. It was knotted with fairy cunning, but at last it came free in his hands, and he withdrew the jeweled pin. As Ethna watched dully, he burned the cloth on the hearth. Next, he gathered the ashes and scattered them outside the castle walls. Then he dealt with the pin.

Even as he tamped the last spadeful of earth into place over the fairy pin, the lord heard running feet and laughter within the castle walls and knew that the spell had lifted. He returned to the hall to see Ethna, flushed and bright-eyed and chattering of the dream she had had. The sojourn with the fairies seemed to her no more than a single night. Her husband smiled and did not reply. Instead, he called for music and food and wine. The wedding revels began anew, and it was as if that year of sorrow had never been.

As the memory of those events was passed down through generations of storytellers, details disappeared: With time, the name of the young lord and even the year of Ethna's abduction were lost. But centuries later, wherever the tale was told – before smoky peat fires in poor peasant huts or in front of opulent blazes in baronial halls – it still drew nods of recognition from its listeners. For the people of that era were well acquainted with the threat and allure of fairyland from their own lives and adventures, and from events near at hand.

In those days, the lives of toiling peasant and leisured noble alike were governed by custom and ritual, but the world was more fluidly defined than it later would be. The year was shaped by the round of the seasons and by the daily cycle of devotion and the annual cycle of festivals established by the Church.

It was in the formal definitions of time that the ambiguity of the age showed the most. A year, for instance, did not necessarily have 365 days. In some countries, Easter began the year. Easter is a movable feast – falling each year on a different Sunday between March 22 and April 25, the date determined by the full of the moon and the day of the vernal equinox – and in those countries, a year could contain eleven, twelve or thirteen months. During that same era, other countries began their years on March 1, following Roman custom; on March 25, the Feast of the Annunciation; or on December 25.

The hours of the day were similarly flexible. Formally, each day was divided into twelve hours of day and twelve of night, which were quartered into three-hour periods. The first hour of the day – called Prime – was dawn; the next marked time was the third hour, Tierce; Sixte was the sixth hour; the ninth, Nones; and the last, Vespers (from the Latin word for evening), which was also the first hour of night. The divisions of time were determined by the Church and announced to everyone by its bells, for no one had clocks to tell the hours.

But the length of an hour changed from day to day: Only at the vernal and autumnal equinoxes are day and night equal in length. At the winter solstice, for instance, daylight might last only six hours, but it still was divided into twelve hours, each thirty minutes long. Even the definitions of the hours changed: Monks were allowed to break their fast at Nones, the ninth hour, which in summer fell at about three o'clock in the afternoon. Driven by hunger, the monastics pushed the ninth hour back to midday, which is why midday came to be called noon.

To the shiftiness of definition was added the uncertainty of life, for the seemly pageant of the ecclesiastical year was played out against a background of chaos, of rude forces that struck at the orderly surface of existence. Hailstorms destroyed harvests and condemned whole countries to winters of want; wars flared on the slimmest of pretexts and left the world in ruins; pestilences savaged the populations at unpredictable intervals.

Given the thinly veiled disorder of the world, it is not surprising that the ungovernable realm of Faerie remained powerful and intrusive and that people observed it with wariness. In its kingdoms and courtly pleasures, Faerie mirrored the mortal world, but it was a realm where time was even less defined. An hour there might last a year in human terms. Change, with its attendant phenomena of growth, fertility and death, was almost unknown: Faerie stood apart from the sorrow and struggle of mortal existence. Yet its inhabitants were endlessly fascinated with humans. Inevitably, the fairies penetrated the world of mortals, disrupting its fragile semblance of order.

Fairy tricks and charms could cast doubt on the most basic certainties. A wanderer who tarried on a Highland moor to listen for a few moments as a hidden songbird trilled a haunting melody might return to his home to find that centuries had passed. Or a farmer's wife, hefting a wheel of cheese to take to market, might find that during the night it had grown as light as a bundle of feathers, its health-giving substance – but not its outward form – charmed away by the fairies.

There were other breakdowns of the natural order in those days, at once more shocking and more intriguing: Unex-

branches of the gorse bushes on the hill. As he looked upon them, they began to dance and tremble: Before his astonished eyes, a cleft opened in the hill, and a band of tiny musicians marched forth piping a rollicking tune. Behind them came a glowing procession of lords and ladies, and servants bearing tables laden with vessels of gold. Fear and avarice battled briefly in the miser's breast, but avarice won.

On hands and knees he stole toward the banquet. He hardly noticed the guards – gnarled creatures called spriggans – who clustered around his knees. They twined his creeping limbs in threadlike ropes and left those ropes slack until the thief raised his hat to clap it over a gold-covered table. At that instant he felt a tug at his legs, and a moment later he was pinned on his back, held fast by a web of threads. "Be the moon gold enough to suit your fancy?" screeched a tiny voice. A spriggan danced on his nose. All that night the miser lay in the dirt, pinched by angry fairy fingers and pricked by a thousand pins.

At dawn the fairies trooped away among the leaves, and the miser struggled free of his gossamer chains. He crept home on aching limbs, and not a word would he say about where he had been. But the village heard the story nonetheless (some said that fairy voices whispered it) and repeated it often and gleefully.

plained disappearances, fits and seizures that left the victim's body intact but abstracted the spirit, babies who changed overnight from pictures of apple-cheeked health and innocence to scrawny imps, as wrinkled as old men, their eyes glittering with a fevered and knowing light. In all of these assaults on the fabric of life, people detected the influence of fairies.

Mortals were not entirely helpless in the face of this uncanny peril. Against kidnapping, a common form of fairy mischief, prudent behavior gave a measure of protection. It was inadvisable, for instance, to step within a circle formed on the ground by mushrooms or one formed by bent stalks of grass. These were fairy rings, marking the boundaries of the other world. It was also unwise to nap on any grassy knoll, for if by chance the hill covered a fairy dwelling, the fairies might swarm out and carry the sleeper to their underground domain.

Ordinary proprieties were also a hedge against fairy abduction; somehow, those mortals who placed themselves at odds with their own society by quarreling or plotting evil deeds were more likely to be snatched into the fairy realm. And, of course, at borderline days and hours – times not even nominally defined for mortals – it was well to be wary.

The consequences of even the most casual brush with fairies could be ruinous, as is shown in the Welsh tale of Taffy ap Sion. Taffy, a shoemaker's son, was a dreamy lad, and when work in his father's shop slackened, he often wandered out among the barren hills and boulder-littered meadows beyond his village, de-

siring nothing more than to be alone with the clouds and the cries of the rooks. His father warned him to stay clear of fairy rings. But Taffy's glance was rarely fixed on the ground, and one blustery afternoon as he wandered, he was startled when the day seemed to brighten suddenly. The next instant, he was deafened by a skirl of high-pitched pipes.

About the Welshman whirled a crowd of men in coats of bottle green and women in gowns of scarlet and white. They were small and comely creatures, and in the searing brightness that enfolded them, they shone like jewels. Banqueting tables stood in their midst, laden with fruit, roast meat and goblets that brimmed and shimmered with ruby wine. All around these tables the flood of merrymakers surged and eddied.

Beyond the circle of brilliance, the mountains and meadows seemed distant and ghostly, as if a heavy mist had descended. Taffy did not care; he had no wish to escape from so carefree and lovely a place. Instead, he clasped hands with two of the revelers and was swept up in the dancing throng.

After five minutes, or perhaps ten, Taffy stumbled and plunged headlong from the fairy ring. He sat on the grass for a moment, his head whirling, marveling that he could neither see nor hear the fairy merrymakers. Then he jumped to his feet. The landscape was transformed. The skyline of crags and ridges was familiar, but where Taffy remembered tussocky grass and hump-backed boulders, the uplands were quilted with verdant fields, edged with stone walls and threaded with lanes.

It was some trick of the fairies, Taffy was certain, but he was uneasy as he set off for home, clambering over unfamiliar and moss-grown walls.

He rounded the hill that shadowed his father's cottage. The house stood where he remembered it – that much was a comfort – but from a hut with a thatched roof and a dusty yard it had grown into a sturdy, slate-roofed farmhouse, shaded by two tall pines. A dog he did not know loped from the doorstep to sniff and bark, and the man who came out to quiet the animal was not Taffy's father, or any neighbor or any kinsfolk.

The farmer, studying the wild-eyed and strangely dressed lad, at first thought the boy was deranged. When Taffy told his story, however, the farmer guessed the truth. He decided to consult an aged woman of the village who knew the lore of the days when the region was sparsely settled – long before the farmer's family had arrived. But as the man led Taffy down the hillside toward the town, the boy's footsteps grew faint, and the man heard a deep sigh. The farmer turned at the sound, and as he watched, Taffy's features blanched and froze, his figure became as tenuous as a ghost's, and then he vanished. A fine shower of black ash filtered to the ground.

It was as the farmer suspected: Minutes had passed within the fairy ring that Taffy danced so happily in, but centuries had rolled by in the mortal world. When Taffy rejoined his fellows and the weight of those years settled at last on his shoulders, he had simply crumbled away. As the old village woman explained to the shaken farmer later, more than 300 years had passed since a shoemaker's son named Taffy ap Sion vanished on the barren mountainside.

The fairies who danced away the centuries with Taffy had made no effort to ensnare him, and they did not try to stop him when he stumbled from their midst. Malice played no part in his downfall, but the realm of the fairies was by nature hostile to the world of mortals, with its inexorable march of hours and days and years. Even the fairies' best intentions could not shelter a human from the cruel consequences of elvish time.

Yet, like everything to do with Faerie, the passage of time there was capricious: Mortals who entered the fairies' world did not necessarily stay for centuries. Peasants talked of captives who were released or rescued from fairy thrall after a year and a day of mortal time, or after seven years – periods that marked likely reopenings of the curtain dividing Faerie from the mortal world. But few who sojourned among the fairies returned unchanged. So complete a break with the order of nature was bound to leave its mark, most often in the form of a consuming desire to return to the alien realm.

A Welsh farm hand named Rhys fell victim to the yearning shortly after he was rescued from a fairy ring. This is how Rhys came to dance with the fairies:

One evening, he and his friend Llewellyn were trudging home from a distant field they had been plowing. Rhys turned to Llewellyn and said that he heard the

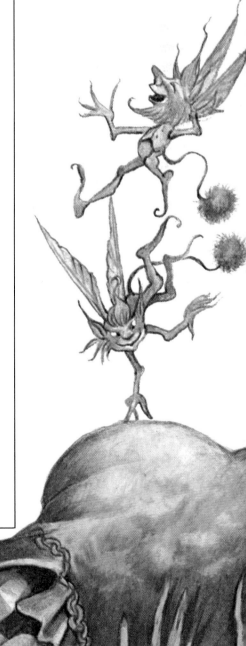

tinkle of harps. The melody was so faint, he told his friend, that it might have been no more than the memory of a song—although he could not say where he had heard it before. It drew him, however, and he left the track for a meadow nearby, telling Llewellyn to go on without him.

Rhys did not return to his village that night or for long afterward, and searchers found no trace of him. A murmur arose in the village that Llewellyn had murdered him and hidden the body. Llewellyn sturdily protested that he was innocent, and finally a villager asked the man to lead him to the spot where Rhys had heard the strange music.

Searching for landmarks in the meadow, Llewellyn discovered among the blackberry bushes a flattened patch of grass. Gingerly he placed one foot on the spot, and at once he found himself on the fringe of a brilliant whirl of fairies, dancing in a cocoon of light. In the center of the ring was Rhys, loose-jointed as a scarecrow, twitching and flailing to the frenzied beat. Keeping one foot planted firmly outside the circle, Llewellyn snagged Rhys's coattails and hauled him from the revels. His village companion was astonished: All he had seen was Llewellyn's curious stance; Rhys seemed to have been pulled out of the air.

Rhys, who believed that he had danced no longer than five minutes, and who heartily resented the interruption, could not resume his old life. He quarreled with friends. He did not work in the fields but wandered alone on the wind-swept uplands, thirsting for the wild music and hearing only the moan of the wind. Weeks

passed this way. Rhys grew gaunt and listless, and one day his solitary figure was no longer seen ranging the hills. At last, a hunter found him dead.

The yearning that afflicted mortals who had tasted the pleasures of Faerie had a counterpart among the fairies, especially in the later centuries of their existence, when the race was dying. They were entranced by mortal vitality and fecundity. In their desire to bring human quickness into their world, they resorted to kidnapping. Their favorite targets were children: sturdy lads, fresh young girls and—most coveted of all—babies.

There is no greater assertion of life than a human infant, and villagers were well aware of the fairy threat to their children. An unbaptized child—having no name to define him and tie him to his world—was at greatest risk, and during the perilous days before christening, a mother might hang from the cradle an opened pair of scissors, meant to play on fairy fears of iron and of the Cross, which the joined blades resembled. The father's trousers, laid inside out across the cradle, could also forestall a fairy raid. So could potent herbs, such as rowan and garlic, tied in little bunches to the sides of the cradle.

No protection against the fairies was guaranteed to work, however. And the worst of it was that a kidnapping might go unnoticed for a while, for the fairies left behind not an empty cradle but a changeling—one of their own number, enchanted briefly into the likeness of the stolen infant. By the time the parents discovered

If on a summer's night a wreath of light glittered on the grass of a meadow, wise mortals drew away. The light was a fairy ring of elfin dancers, and the man or maid who stepped within its glow would be imprisoned in their world.

that there was something amiss, the fairies were safe in their own land, chittering over their prize.

No fairy changeling could feign the vitality of a child for long. Deception was hampered all the more by the fact that the substitute was usually an aged member of the fairy tribe, happy to be pampered by a mortal mother but unable to permanently conceal his scrawny and mottled hideousness. And the common people had an arsenal of tests for a suspected changeling. Many were cruel ordeals: The infant might be placed on a shovel and held over a fire, or it might be left on a dunghill all day, exposed to the weather.

If the child was indeed a fairy in disguise, the outcome was happy: The instant that torture was threatened, the elf would shed its mortal likeness, cackle and vanish, while from the cradle would come the cry of the mother's true baby, whom the fairies always returned when their deed was revealed. But if the child was no changeling—and babies who failed to thrive or were transformed overnight by illness often fell under suspicion—the effect of a trial by fire or exposure could be tragic. Fortunately, there were gentler ways to unmask a changeling, and they were effective, as an Irish tale shows.

A certain woman was awakened one morning by an unfamiliar clamor: Her baby boy, until that day robust and placid, was hoarse with sobbing. She hurried to his cradle, then drew back in shock. His cheeks, full the day before, had withered and fallen, his skin was as papery as an old man's, and every bone started from his tiny ravaged form. She called her neighbors, and although some thought a fever had wasted her child during the night, most agreed that this was an instance of fairy mischief.

The traditional village remedies were harsh. Sear the imp over the flames, they said, or cast it into a snowbank: The fairy changeling will disappear at once and before long your proper child will be given back to you. The woman could not bring herself to follow their advice. Squall as it might, the creature did look like a ghost of her own baby boy.

A wise neighbor had more measured counsel. "There is a way to learn the truth without doing harm," she said. The mother, eager for help, still could not keep her eyes from widening as the old woman described her remedy.

"You want to give him a little surprise," she advised. "Set a caldron of water on the fire to boil; then get a dozen new-laid eggs, break them and throw away all but the shells. When the water begins to steam, toss in the eggshells and say that you are brewing ale from them, and then you will know whether the child in the cradle is your boy or a fairy. If it is a fairy," she added casually, "you can slip a red-hot poker down its throat, and that fairy will trouble you no more."

Soon the mother was seated at her hearth, a pot of water at a merry boil on the turf fire and a basket of eggs by her side. For once, the cradle was silent. She picked up the eggs one by one and cracked them, pouring the liquid into a bucket and arranging the shells in a row on the

Sometimes even as a mortal mother watched, her baby in its cradle
shriveled into a puling gargoyle. Then the mother knew the truth:
Fairies had stolen her child and left a changeling in its place.

hearth. She dropped the shells into the pot; then she heard the cracked voice of an old man behind her. "What are you doing, Mammy?" it asked.

The mother turned to meet eyes that were glittering and alien. The wizened infant sat bolt upright in the cradle. Her doubts fast dissolving, the woman thrust the poker into the fire. "I'm brewing, my son," she answered.

"And what are you brewing, Mammy?"

"Eggshells, my boy," she said, with a glance at the poker.

"Oh," shrieked the imp, rising to its feet in the wildly swinging cradle, "I'm fifteen hundred years old, and I never saw a brewery of eggshells before."

The woman could not wait; the still-cool poker could bludgeon if it could not burn. She seized it and made for the fairy, but when she reached the cradle she saw that a soft, round form swelled the covers: Her own child was there safe and sound, without so much as a scratch.

Some authorities guessed that the fairies' delight in healthy infants arose not just from a fascination with the vigor of humankind but also from a concrete need: To bolster their frail and ancient lineage with an infusion of human stock. Whatever the truth of the matter, it was certain that the fairies had specific uses for the strengths and talents of mortal adults. Midwives often were briefly summoned to assist in fairy births, and wet nurses were carried off to suckle fairy children—for if fairy mothers gave milk at all, it must have been thin and unwholesome stuff. The fairies also abducted humans for domestic servants, to cook and carry and clean.

Mortals who were rescued from fairy servitude rarely suffered the deadly longing that afflicted those who danced and feasted with the fairies as equals. It was as if only the willing participation in fairy delights bound a mortal to fairyland. Unwilling visitors to Faerie often discovered that the glittering surface of some fairies' lives was no more than an illusion covering a reality that was dust and ashes. Mortals whose vision pierced the illusion—commonly known as fairy glamor—felt no desire to remain in the other world. Like purloined children, captive adults generally returned from fairy bondage with their spirits unscathed.

But their rescue was a daunting task, for the elfin kidnappers of an adult rarely left behind a changeling. At most, the fairies placed in the bed of the victim a so-called stock, a wooden likeness of the prisoner that was animated, for a few days, with a

From time to time, anxious mortal mothers said, bands of trooping elves raided country
hamlets, stealing healthy human infants to strengthen the dwindling fairy stock.

magical semblance of life. When the fairy glamor wore off and the stock grew still and rigid, relatives usually assumed that their loved one had died, never suspecting the fairy ruse.

Providing the kidnapping was detected, there always remained the hope of rescue. But, as was the case with an Irish farmer who lost his wife to the fairies, luck tended to play a role.

The farmer was a sound sleeper, and he first learned of his wife's disappearance when he was roused in the morning by his baby as it wailed for milk from its cradle at the foot of the bed. The man reached over to wake his wife. He found her place empty and cold. At the door of the bedroom stood two older children, wide-eyed and fearful, for they had witnessed their mother's departure.

In the depths of the night, they had been awakened by light that spilled from the door of their parents' bedroom. The children had crept to the door and had seen their mother gliding toward them as if in a trance, treading in a pool of light amid a crowd of men who glowed like shards of stained glass. The brother and sister called to their mother, but she passed them without turning.

After hearing this account, the farmer left his weeping children and went around his village, questioning each of his neighbors. It was as he had expected: None had seen his Molly, and all supposed that she was with the fairies. During the days and weeks that followed, the heartsick farmer could only wait and hope.

One morning the village midwife came to him with news. The night before, she said, a dark gentleman had rapped at her door, agitated as any prospective father. At moments like that, she said, she asked no questions. She had simply gathered her things into a bundle and mounted behind the man on his glossy black horse.

As the horse lunged into a gallop, the midwife held on tight and closed her eyes. The journey was short, and when the midwife opened her eyes, she found herself in a sumptuous chamber, hung with tapestries and warm from the blaze leaping on the hearth. At the center of the chamber stood a vast, canopied bed, and almost lost beneath the covers lay a delicate lady, with features of chiseled beauty twisted by the pain of labor.

The midwife's skilled hands soon held a baby boy, purple and bawling, and the dark man came in with a pot of ointment for her to rub into the infant's skin. After she had finished her work, she brushed her right eye with a greasy finger. At once it seemed as if the sight of that eye had dimmed. The splendid chamber had dwindled to an oozy cave, the bed to a shelf of rock covered with straw, and the blazing logs to a mound of smoldering turf. Then she knew that she had attended the birth of a fairy child.

The midwife had heard before of fairy ointments that endowed a mortal eye with fairy sight. It startled her, nonetheless, to see the fairies so withered and sharp-faced. A baby as scrawny as a plucked chicken rested on its mother's flaccid breast. And the ointment revealed another surprise: In the shadows, where a great candelabra had stood, waited buxom Molly, gesturing anxiously.

The fairy father left the chamber for a moment, and the midwife hurried to Molly's side. Molly said that she had been captured to suckle the fairy infant and thought never to see home again. But now she sensed a chance of rescue, made possible by the midwife's accidental gaining of fairy sight. "Wait with my husband at the edge of town next Friday, just before midnight," she told the midwife. "You will see the fairies pass in procession, with me among them. Guide my husband to me, and if he holds me tight no matter what, he will have me back again."

The fairy father announced that he would convey the midwife back to her village. His horse, formerly a beautiful animal, looked like a ragwort stalk to her, but she feared to betray her new-found fairy sight, so she mounted obediently. Through the blackness and tumult of the night, she was spirited to her doorstep.

So ended the midwife's tale. She gave the farmer a penetrating look. "Now you know what you must do," she said.

Accordingly, that Friday night the husband and the midwife waited at the edge of the village. As midnight approached, the midwife tightened her grip on the farmer's arm. The pebbles on the lane began to stir and rattle under the tread of feet invisible to the farmer but not to his companion. The farmer heard garments rustle like the wind through dead leaves. Then the midwife shoved him. The farmer lurched forward and closed his arms around a soft, familiar form.

At once he was beset by phantoms. The moonlit landscape vanished behind curtains of flame, and the roar of a conflagration sounded in his ears. The leaping flames divided themselves into glowing arrows that soared high into the blackness and then plunged earthward. They lanced the ground at the farmer's feet, and from the wounded earth poured a glistening black mass of malignant creatures, impossible to identify in the gloom. They hopped and quivered toward the farmer's legs, and he shut his eyes and steeled himself for their poisonous touch. But it did not come. The form stirred within his embrace, and when he opened his eyes the terrors had vanished, and he saw beside him his Molly, blinking as if awaking from a long sleep.

Only the midwife met fairies again. In the market of her village, she was startled to see, through her right eye, the same wizened fairy who had summoned her to the birth of his son. He was stepping lightly through the crowd, casually pilfering cheeses and sausages from the stalls. She shouted angrily at him, and he looked up in surprise. Then he walked over to her, and all the way around her, trying to determine which eye it was that saw him. At last he was sure, and he jabbed his finger, its nail as sharp as a rose thorn, into the midwife's right eye, blinding it.

*C*ourage came naturally to Molly's husband, for he loved his wife. But he had a model for his steadfastness. Storytellers in villages like the farmer's told of an earlier time—the days of Ethna and of the Tuatha Dé Danann—when men of heroic stature walked the earth, and the fairies, too, were wreathed in a glory that

With a harp that sang of wonders and of love that never faltered, King Orfeo of Thrace
forced an elfin lord to free his wife, who had been long a captive by fairy enchantments.

the world has not seen since. Their beauty was no false product of glamor, but innate, and they were as bold and passionate as any human knight. The fairy kings who abducted mortal women at that time took them not as servants and nurses but as wives or lovers, or to add to the splendor of their domains. Many another knight besides Ethna's husband had to wrest his lady from a fairy challenger. It was these brave and loving mortals, perhaps, that the farmer recalled as he waited that night by the moonlit lane. He may have known, as many people knew, the tale of Orfeo.

Famed for his harp-playing as well as for his just and loving nature, Orfeo reigned in Thrace, in northern Greece. His rule was a time of prosperity and peace for courtiers and commonfolk alike. But those halcyon days ended one afternoon in May when Orfeo's lovely Queen, Heurodis, was carried in from the palace garden, shaken and sobbing.

At length she told her story. That morning, birdsong and the gentle spring air had lulled her to sleep under an ymp tree – that is, a tree formed not by nature but by grafting. Perhaps because these trees were a kind of disordering of natural processes, they often marked borders between the mortal and the Faerie realms, and Heurodis had been careless indeed to linger near one. At noon, a border line of time, she had awakened with a start.

Heurodis had dreamed that she would soon be parted from Orfeo and from the whole bright world. A Fairy King, tall and gleaming and wearing a crown ablaze with gems, had approached and wordlessly gathered her in his arms. He had carried her through darkness to his own land, where he showed her turreted castles and flowery meadows and soaring flocks of white birds. Then the King set her down beneath the ymp tree again and, on pain of dreadful punishment, ordered her to wait for him there the next day. She dared not defy him, she told Orfeo.

The next morning, Orfeo mustered his knights and surrounded the tree where Heurodis waited, pale and silent. As they stood gazing around for some sign of a hostile force, only the clank of their armor and the jingle of bridles broke the midday calm. Suddenly, Orfeo, standing guard nearest the tree, gave a cry. Heurodis had disappeared from the very center of the ring of armed men.

Overcome by sorrow, Orfeo abandoned his throne and fled to the wilderness, taking with him only his harp. For ten years he stilled his hunger with roots, berries and bark. He pillowed his head at night on stones, under the stars when the weather was fair and in caves when it rained or snowed. He grew gaunt and shaggy, and his sole pleasure was in his music. When the harp's plangent notes floated through the forest, songbirds fell silent, and wild beasts rustled the undergrowth as they crept near to listen.

Orfeo met no other mortal during those long years of wandering, but on hot summer days, he saw glinting fairy cavalcades threading through the high grass of forest meadows and heard the distant blasts of their hunting horns. One day he awoke to the crack of sticks and the thump of hoofbeats on the forest floor. Emerging from the shadows was a procession of fairy huntresses, each mounted on a snowy horse, each with a silver-gray falcon resting on a gloved hand. One of the ladies turned to look at the poor minstrel that Orfeo had become, and that one was Heurodis. They gazed at each other and their eyes brimmed with tears. But before they could speak, the procession had moved on.

Casting aside all caution, Orfeo seized his harp and followed the huntresses into the forest. When a cliff loomed up before them, they wound through a cleft into the very rock. Orfeo kept close behind, guided through the blackness by the clatter of hoofs. He groped for hours along a tortuous corridor; then light stung his eyes, and he was dazzled by a white-towered castle that rose from a verdant plain.

All gates open for a wandering minstrel, and Orfeo soon gained entrance to the castle. Within its walls, he passed through gardens littered with sleeping mortals, all positioned just as they had been at the instant the fairies carried them off. Here and there, like equestrian statues, were mounted knights, spirited away from the mortal world at the height of conflict. Orfeo found the Fairy King in the central courtyard—and there lay Heurodis, asleep under a tree that was the mirror of the one in her own palace garden.

Orfeo knelt before the Fairy King and offered to play. The fairy, raising his brows at the humble appearance of the minstrel, grudgingly agreed. But when a cascade of shimmering notes poured from the harp strings, the King's demeanor softened. Orfeo's melody quivered and died. And the mighty Fairy King offered any reward the minstrel might ask.

"Then give me," Orfeo answered, "that lady who sleeps under the ymp tree."

"An unseemly match," replied the King. "It would be a loathsome thing to see her in your company."

"It would be more loathsome still for you to have lied when you offered me any reward," answered Orfeo.

That was true, as the King knew. He gestured, and Heurodis stirred and wakened. Her gaze fell on her husband, and her pale face brightened. In an instant she was beside him. Orfeo took her hand and led her from the hall. And although some chroniclers claim that he lost her during the long, dark passage back through the wall of rock separating the fairy from the mortal realm, others say that Orfeo and Heurodis returned to the world of daylight in triumph and were crowned anew.

In later times, those who heard of Orfeo and his journey to fairyland were stirred by his triumph as if it had been their own. For in his tale they saw mirrored their own fears of the fairy realm and its cruel intrusions into the world of mortals. Yet, if fairyland was a threat for most of humankind, a few mortals, set apart from their fellows by godlike powers or by the love of a fairy maiden, found in the fairy domain a refuge from death.

Among these fortunate few—a legend-veiled company said to include King Arthur—was Thomas the Rhymer, a poet and dreamer of Scotland. His countrymen first knew of his traffic with the fairies when Thomas wandered into the marketplace at Ercildoune, his native hamlet, after an

Summoned by the sweet airs that Thomas the Rhymer sang in a lonely wood, an elf Queen rode from her world into his. She took the mortal man with her into Faerie, and there he lived for seven years.

absence of seven years. The villagers had long since given him up for dead, and he answered their insistent questions with a strange tale.

He told of a Fairy Queen who, seven years before, had ridden from among the trees as he lay plucking his lute, in a wood outside Ercildoune. The Queen smiled and drew rein before him; she was as lovely as the dawn, and he played sweet and artful melodies to win her. At last she dismounted, and he made to kiss her. She warned him that the act would bind him to her for seven years, but his heart thrilled with love, and he did not hesitate. Then she climbed on her white horse, wheeled, and with Thomas close behind on foot, set off at an easy canter for another world.

Their journey took them through perpetual night, where an ocean of blood seethed about Thomas' knees, across an inky heath and into a bright meadow. There the Fairy Queen showed Thomas a manicured path, broad and well-worn, that led to perdition, and a steep, narrow way, choked with briars, that was the way of righteousness. "But for singers and lovers of beauty such as we," she said, "there is a third way." And she led him along a gentle, twisting path, where their steps were hushed by moss and their legs caressed by encroaching ferns. It was the way to fairyland.

And now that the appointed period was up, the Fairy Queen had sent Thomas back to Ercildoune to live out his span. When the hubbub of his return died away, Thomas resumed the life of an earthbound mortal. But his poems sang with new eloquence and his prophecies brought him renown, for in fairyland he had eaten an apple whose flesh held the power of truth – a parting gift from the Fairy Queen.

During his time in the mortal world, it was Thomas' habit to host each year a banquet for kinsfolk and villagers. Strange tidings interrupted the feast that was held in his seventy-eighth year. A crofter's lad hurried into the hall, and silence fell as the boy stammered his news. A pair of milk white deer, hart and hind, were trotting down the lane toward the house of the poet, he reported. The villagers were unnerved by the report. Surely Thomas, the wisest man in the land, would know what these unnatural creatures signified.

Thomas thanked the boy and rose. "They are come from the fairy world," he told his guests, "and I must follow them." He strode from the hall.

In the lane, a silent throng of villagers saw the deer pause at Thomas' approach, then fall into place at his side. Only the crunch of Thomas' footsteps sounded as the prophet, his otherworldly companions beside him, paced the length of the village and out into the forest that enclosed it. The little procession flickered briefly behind the dark pines; then it vanished.

So, as his mortal life drew to a close, Thomas the Rhymer was called back to fairyland. If the reports of later visitors to that realm are to be trusted, he dwells there still, beguiling the fairies with poetry and song and guiding them with his counsel. Thus, in the company of his fairy lover, Thomas overcame mortality and the death of earthly love. Few other mortals, even among those who loved fairy maidens, have equaled his good fortune.

Forbidden fare

Among the many dangers posed by the fairy world was that of eating elvish food. It was said that doing so made mortals partake of the fairy nature and thus trapped them forever in fairyland. It was also said that one taste of the food made mortals pine for a second, and that the pining could kill them.

A British poet sang of two sisters who lived near a glen where a company of elves held a nightly market, offering plump pears and plums, blossomy peaches and silvered grapes. Although this market was usually invisible, the sisters glimpsed it one night. The elder sister fled, but the younger girl lingered. The fairies beckoned her greedily, and in exchange for a lock of her hair they gave her all the sweet fruit she could eat.

Drunk with the juices, she reeled home at last, now stricken with longing for the pretty poison. Night after night she went to the glen, but the market had disappeared. And so she wasted away, tortured by her craving.

When it became clear that the girl was dying, the elder sister acted. She went alone to the glen. Sensing a fresh victim, the fairies displayed their seductive wares, but these they would sell only on the condition that she eat with them. Having no wish for the fairy affliction, the maiden refused. The elves danced with rage. In a moment they surrounded her, pinching and biting, clawing and screeching. They crushed their fruit against her face to force her to eat, but the girl stood firm, lips tightly closed while her cheeks were smeared with juices.

Dawn came at last, and with it surcease. The fairies disappeared, chittering angrily. The girl made her way home to her ailing sister and commanded a kiss. That kiss gave the younger girl a taste of the juices that syruped her sister's face. Her longing was satisfied – and the second taste cured it. She began to bloom anew.

So the sisters lived happily for many years. But neither ventured near that glen again.

Tam Lin

The rescue of a mortal from the grasp of captor fairies
was a venture fraught with danger. Few people were
steadfast enough for the attempt, but there were
some. One was a Scotswoman, the daughter of the
Earl of March. Janet was her name.

Near the castle where she lived, just north of the
English border, was a place called Carterhaugh Wood,
known to be guarded by an elfin knight. No maiden
went there and returned unscathed, but Janet cared
not a whit for the danger. Early one summer afternoon
she left her father's hall and went blithely to a well in
the wood, to pluck the briar roses there. She picked
one—and the knight appeared before her in the leafy
shade, tall and pale and cloaked in silk.

The setting sun had begun to send shafts of gold
through the leaves before Janet left that wood,

a maid no more. But she went again another day to find the knightly stranger, for she had loved him at once. In the drowsy summer afternoons, he told her what he was—no elf, but as mortal as she. His name was Tam Lin, and he was the grandson of the Earl of Roxburgh, captured by the fairies years before. He had served the Fairy Queen since, guarding her wood by day and riding with her troop by night.

What mortal could rescue Tam Lin from that shadow life but Janet who loved him? She told him she would save him if she could, and Tam Lin described how the mortal must challenge the power of the Fairy Queen. Then he faded into the sun-speckled forest. On the Eve of Allhallows, following Tam Lin's instructions, Janet stole through the moonlit wood to a crossroads nearby—an in-

between place, where fairies might be
seen — and hid herself behind a thorn hedge. At midnight she heard the trills of music pipes and the
softer notes of lyres; she saw a glow, as of throngs of
fireflies, suffusing the sky just beyond the crossroads.

With jingling bridles and pealing bells, the fairy
troop came into view. At its head, riding tall on a
black horse, was the Queen, her countenance as pale
as an image seen in an antique glass. Lords and ladies
followed, their delicate, ghostly faces turned up toward the moonlight, their elfin locks flowing behind.

At last, in that uncertain light, Janet saw Tam Lin
and knew him by the signs he had given her in Carterhaugh Wood: He rode a moon-white horse; he wore
only one gauntlet, and on his brow rested a golden
circlet. As Tam Lin had bade her, Janet acted. When
he came abreast of her, she sprang
fearlessly from

her hiding place and dragged him from the saddle. At once a shrill, fierce fairy cry rang out: "Tam Lin is away!" The Queen reined in her horse, swiveled in her saddle and fixed Tam Lin with an icy gaze.

The knight's warm body seemed to melt in Janet's grasp. She clutched empty air and thought Tam Lin was lost. But he was not: Tiny feet beat against her palm and a salamander writhed in an effort at escape. With an instinct quicker than thought, Janet cupped her hands and contained the creature. The elfin Queen's eyes glittered, and the salamander swelled until Janet found herself holding the cold, scaly coils of a serpent that flexed and twined about her arms and neck. She set her jaw and pressed herself against the creature, clutching it in a lover's embrace while a numbing chill crept through her heart. Janet did not flinch or slacken, for the knight had told her what her trial would be: All that could save him from his enchantment was the unyielding grasp of a mortal lover, given at midnight on Allhallows Eve. The Fairy Queen cried out, and the scales under Janet's hands melted away, to be replaced by the thick fur and shining teeth of a bear. Janet trembled, but she held her breath against the beast's rank odor and stood fast, her

arms grasping its massive body. With a cry of rage, the Fairy Queen lifted her arm, and all around, Janet heard a sound as of sails flapping in the wind. Straining against her grip was a swan, its bill pecking sharply at her face, its great wings beating against her arms. But the mortal grasp never weakened. And at last the struggling stopped. Where serpent, beast and bird had fought was only a heavy iron bar — but that bar was incandescent with its heat, burning the mortal flesh. It was the end, and Janet knew it. Dodging the trampling hoofs of the fairy horses and closing her ears against the eldritch cries, she ran into the Caterhaugh Wood and cast the iron into the well. There was a hiss of steam as the

bar struck the water, then silence. From the well
stepped a naked man—Tam Lin, reborn into the
mortal world. Janet wrapped him in her cloak.

Behind them was the elfin Queen, steadying her
dancing horse and regarding them with cold
eyes. The battle was over. "Had I but known
that an earthly woman would win you away with her
love, Tam Lin," she cried, "I would have taken out
your heart of flesh and given you one of stone." She
wheeled and summoned her company to her, and then
the fairy band faded like wraiths into the trees.

But Tam Lin and Janet scarcely heard, the chroniclers say—their thoughts were only for mortal love.

Chapter Four

The Heart's Far-Carrying Call

In the season of mists, when the earth was white with hoarfrost and the trees gleamed bare and black, a solitary knight wandered the Kentish hills. He was a young man, but his gait was shambling and slow. Once he had been comely; now his bones stretched the pale skin of his face, and his eyes were sunk in shadows. The knight had been brought to this pass by an encounter during the summer of that year. The land was blooming then: The meadows were carpeted with primrose and heartsease, and the air was laden with the scent of lavender. One bright morning, he set out for London to join the King's armies. He rode briskly at first, but the country lanes were warm and quiet, save for the blackbird's song and the echoing notes of the cuckoo, and soon the knight's horse slowed to a walk. The young man rode on unheeding, drowsily dreaming his young man's dreams. After some time, his reverie was broken by a fluttering movement near an oak beside the lane. He spoke, but no one replied. Made foolhardy by curiosity, he dismounted and strode to the tree.

"Come out," he said.

A trill of laughter was the only reply.

"Come out," called the knight again.

A woman stepped lightly into the lane and stood before him. She seemed clothed with the dawn, for her draperies were the color of rose petals, and she was crowned with a cascade of fiery hair. She met the knight's stare with green cat eyes as shy as any forest creature's, and in that instant, the knight was lost. Every thought of king and country faded into that gaze.

Without speaking a word, he held out his arms to the fairy. She came quite willingly, it seemed, and the knight lifted her to the saddle of his horse. In a language he could not understand, she whispered to the animal, which turned obediently from the path and, with the knight pacing alongside, threaded its way through the trees and into the sunny meadows that lay beyond.

They traveled thus for hours, now in field and now in shady forest. From time to time, the lady spoke softly. The knight plucked wild flowers for her, and with nimble fingers, she fashioned them into garlands for her blazing hair. When the sun stood high in the heavens, she began to sing, weaving a net of melodies around the man who walked beside her. She leaned from the saddle and peered into his eyes with a look of such absorbing tenderness that he could not speak for longing.

At last, when the afternoon was well advanced, the lady spoke a word in her strange tongue, and the horse halted in a small elder copse. The knight lifted her from the saddle and looked again into her face. He saw inexpressible sadness. Tears glistened in the green eyes and glittered on the lashes. The knight kissed the fairy then, but she drew herself from his arms and once more began to sing. Light as morning mist, the voice coiled around him, and the young man's eyes grew heavy. He swayed and sank to the ground. He saw for a moment the rosy draperies of the lady and the bright tendrils of her hair, swinging as she bent to watch him; above her head, the canopy of leaves wheeled. He closed his eyes.

As he slept, he dreamed of darkness. He saw a line of men, knights like himself, but haggard and gray in death. Their dry lips were split over gaping black mouths, and shadows filled their empty eye sockets. The lips moved, and the knight realized that the ghostly figures were calling his name. Their bony fingers waved, summoning him.

He awakened bathed in icy sweat, staring up through the leaves at the stars. He was alone. He sighed and closed his eyes and slept again.

Dawn came, and the knight's second waking, and with it a premonition of dreadful grief. The fairy was gone, having taken his heart from his breast. He knew that she had left him as surely as if he had seen her die. He knew that from then on, every hour would be achingly empty. His fate had come upon him – a life full of yearning that never would be satisfied, of calling and hearing no reply.

Sick with desire, he rose and searched. He hunted through the copse but found no sign of the fairy. He paced the meadows, following every path and byway, and still he found no sign.

So that first day passed and the next and the next. The flowers faded in the fields, the harvests were gathered in and the birds ceased their singing. Still the knight wandered, a gaunt figure silhouetted against the winter sky, a man bereft of hope but not of longing.

At last he could walk no farther. He lay down on the bracken. The final earthly sounds he heard were the moan of the wind and the hoarse cries of quarreling rooks. In that hour, he died.

The countrymen who found the wasted body said little, but their faces were set and grim. When they were safe in their homes again, they whispered of fairy enchantments and of the ranks of mortals who were victims of fairy love. They spoke with fear, as mortals often did when they talked of the powers of Faerie.

Yet, in those distant days, the current of love between the mortal and the fairy realms ran deep and strong. Impelled by longing, mortals and fairies both strove to breach the boundaries that separated them, and sometimes they succeeded. But not even passion and affection were sufficient to keep open the invisible walls between the worlds. Ever desiring, human and fairy were ever divided. The stories of their loves were almost always pervaded by sorrow and filled with the pain of loss.

Mortal customs did not help, for they were weighted against strangers and strangeness. Among mortals in those dangerous times, the only certain trust was in kinship. The names of their fathers or mothers identified men and women and showed their place in the hierarchy of a family. In Celtic countries, carefully recorded blood ties spread in ever-widening circles. The Welsh, for instance, understood relationships to the ninth degree — that is to say, to the position of third cousin once removed or of great-great-great-great-great-great-great-grandparent — and the Irish to the seventeenth. An outsider who injured one member of a family clan was answerable to all of its members to specified degrees, and all of them could exact appropriate vengeance.

The importance of blood kinship was such that marriage among mortals posed a special problem — that of safely admitting into a family a bride or groom who did not share its blood. In earliest times, the stranger was surrounded by all sorts of conditions that indicated his alien status. Wives might go through life forbidden to call their husbands by name, for instance, since the mention of it gave power to the speaker. Women used such epithets as "My Master" instead. And in those places where husbands joined their wives' families, the grooms were hedged about with rules of behavior that set them apart: They might be forbidden to speak to their wives' relatives, or be required to live in the household in special, separate quarters.

In later, safer times, of course, more comfortable arrangements prevailed; but throughout Europe, wedding customs continued to reflect the sense that a stranger entering a family carried about him something of a threat. In Ireland and Wales, weddings were celebrated with mock battles during which the groom's party – in the role of enemy, for the moment – attacked the party of the bride and spirited her away; the role of best man was originally that of groom's strong right arm in the abduction. (Among the Irish, the ride to the wedding feast that followed such a battle was referred to as "dragging home the bride.") Or, in an echo of half-forgotten barriers, mock trials were set for the groom who desired a bride: In Brittany, relatives disguised themselves as the wished-for maiden; the prospective groom's task was to identify her properly. In Wales and Russia the trial was often the answering of riddles.

Given the distrust of outsiders, mortals' fear of fairy lovers was unsurprising. A fairy, after all, belonged to a separate race entirely, one whose nature was variable and even perverse. Entrancing in their beauty, fairies extended a powerful claim on the human heart – yet the love of some of them brought only death, as it did for the Kentish knight and the knights whom that fairy had ensnared before him.

Not all such death-bringers were as complex as the Kentish temptress, who wept at the fate her nature made inevitable. Among the Irish, for instance, there was a fairy called the *leanan-side* – or "fairy mistress" – who drifted through villages and towns at night, battening on amorous young men. When they entered her embrace, however, life and breath drained from them, while the fairy grew bright and strong.

European countryfolk knew that forests, streams and pools sheltered appealing but destructive fairies such as the *vile*

and the nixes. In Russia, infinitely desirable and infinitely dangerous fairies called *rusalky* inhabited rivers and lakes. They sat upon the shores, combing their hair in the moonlight and smiling secret and seductive smiles. No man, it was said, was proof against one. Even ascetic monks were found drowned in the waters where *rusalky* trailed their pretty fingers.

But fairies of both sexes might deal in fatal love. The water nixes of Germany, for example, had male counterparts. And from the British Isles came tales of elfin seducers whose power over women was very strong indeed.

The Irish, for instance, spoke of the Ganconer, a debonair elf who might appear to maidens so unwise as to venture alone into the wild. The pipe that he smoked was his hallmark and a warning to women, but even those who knew of this were seduced by his gleaming black eyes and his caressing voice, speaking the sweet words that gave the elf his name – which meant "Love Talker." A woman who yielded to the Ganconer's whispers and kissed him was lost. "Who meets the Love Talker," ran the Irish saying, "must weave her shroud soon." And it was true. After his interludes with mortal women, the elf would disappear, satisfied for a time. The mortals always pined and died.

Another such fairy – the subject of many a Scottish song – was an elfin knight known as the demon lover. He was once betrothed to a mortal but left her for seven years (why he did so is not known). Before he left, she promised fidelity. She married a mortal in his absence, however.

When the demon lover reappeared, he

Love's last embrace

Graceful enchantresses of river, brook and pool, the *rusalky* of Russia were reputed to be murderers of men, seducing their victims to a watery demise. Some *rusalky*, however, loved mortals, and one even left her lake to marry a prince.

There was a condition to that union: She could stay among mortals only so long as her husband remained faithful. In time, he betrayed her, as mortals will, and the distraught fairy returned to her home. But the prince, filled with remorse, sought her out. When he called from the verge of her pool, she came at once. He knelt to embrace her. She warned him that – doomed as she now was to keep to the liquid element – she had become a danger: The embrace of a *rusalka* brought only death.

Yet the prince gathered her into loving arms and kissed her – and died. Widowed by her fairy nature, the *rusalka* was left to mourn for all eternity.

reproached the woman bitterly – and then seduced her. She deserted her husband and her infant children to follow the elf to a ship he had waiting for her, a fine galleon with sails of taffeta and masts of beaten gold. She could see no crew, but the fairy's thrall held her, and she followed him aboard. At once the wind rose, and the galleon skimmed across the sea. When it was three leagues from shore, the demon lover struck the topmast once and the foremast once. The beautiful ship cracked and sank, carrying the faithless woman to a grave on the ocean floor.

The demon lover's vengefulness, while harsh, was at least understandable in human terms. Throughout northern Europe, however, lived elfin knights who existed only to destroy. Maidens who crossed into their enchanted territories found themselves as helpless as the mortal victim of the demon lover. Sometimes the knights only seduced the maidens – but the loss of a woman's honor was a serious

Just before the full moon rose, wild swans settled on mountain pools and swam there until the evening deepened. Then they stepped from the water and shed their swan forms to dance in the moonlight as maidens.

fate in those days. More often, the elves murdered the mortals.

Still, if songs and tales from Germany, Scandinavia and Scotland are to be credited, the power of those elfin knights could be combated. One woman who refused to succumb was Isabel the Fair, who lived at her father's court in the north of Scotland long ago.

On the morning of the first day of May, Isabel sat alone in her bower, busy at her embroidery. Far away and faint across the hills, she heard a horn of elfland (a sound so sweet could be no other). The wild call trembled in the air, and the maiden's flashing needle paused. An image came to her, a vision of shining castle walls and still lakes, and of an elfin knight astride a mighty charger.

"If I but had that knight to sleep beside me," whispered Isabel the Fair. . . . But her thought was never finished.

It was unwise to wish when the sound from the other world had yet to die. Before her needle plunged again, a princely man appeared in the courtyard beneath Isabel's window; he was riding a tall horse and leading a pretty palfrey. He raised his head and smiled upon her gravely.

"Isabel the Fair," said the man, "you called and I have come for you. Ride into the greenwood with me now." The palfrey tossed its head, and the bells on its harness rang merrily.

The needle and embroidery silk slipped to the floor. Isabel sped down a winding stone stair and into the courtyard. With-

out a word she mounted the palfrey, and together she and the elf clattered across the cobblestones and out through the castle gate. As they galloped across the hills, no word was said between them. Finally, they came to a wood, and there the elfin knight drew up. He leaned from his saddle and took the palfrey's reins from her.

"Isabel the Fair," said he, "dismount now. You have come to the place where you are to die."

She stared at him. He returned her gaze with one as calm as a mountain pool.

"I have slain seven kings' daughters here, Isabel the Fair," said he. "You are to be the eighth." His voice was gentle, his eyes clear and blank. Isabel slid from the saddle to the ground, and he swung down beside her. He slapped the horses' flanks, and the animals ambled into the forest, reins trailing.

Suddenly Isabel smiled. She stroked the knight's sleeve with a small, soft hand and in her sweet voice bade him lie down with her, that she might rest before she died. And he did that. Isabel sat in the grass of the greenwood and held his head in her lap and stroked his hair. In her mind, she recited a charm, one that her mother had taught her for bringing on sleep, and sleep he did.

After a while, she carefully unbuckled his belt, pulled it off and bound it around his body just above the elbows, so his arms were strapped to his sides. Then she waited for the power of her simple spell to fade. At length, the knight stirred, his heavy head lolling across her knees. He opened his eyes and looked up at her drowsily, and in that instant she moved. She stabbed him in the heart with his own dagger.

He made no move or sound when the bloody stain spread across his breast, but the light faded from his eyes. Isabel watched until they dulled; then she shifted herself from under him.

"If seven kings' daughters you here have slain," said she, "then lie here a husband to them all." She rose, turned her back on the stiffening elf and began her long walk home. That is the last that is known of the Scotswoman, whose walk from the greenwood took her out of history.

But to dwell on Isabel and her kind — or on the perils mortals faced in seeking fairy love — is to distort the story, for it ignores the mortals and fairies who sought each other not simply with amorous intent, but with steadfast and faithful love. They found — before they met the fate that governed their loving — the perfect comfort of companioned hearts.

Thus it was with mortal men who fell in love with swans — birds so splendid that they were admired from the dawn of history and in every country of the world. The race of swans was held in

such awe that in lands as far apart as Russia and Ireland, it was said that to kill one of them would bring death to the killer. For swans were beings of Faerie sojourning in the mortal world, as some mortals learned to their joy and sorrow.

A Norwegian chronicler tells this tale: A huntsman once rested beside a mountain lake as night approached. All was quiet except for the lisping of the water at the lake's edge. Then, barely audible in the air, the huntsman heard a ringing trill — the lovely sound called wing music, made by the mute swan in flight.

The huntsman looked up. High above was the flock, tiny specks growing rapidly larger as the birds began their descent. They wheeled in a gyre of white like the whorls of a seashell, each in turn settling onto the waters of the lake. There they floated in the swan's graceful fashion, inclining their long necks to watch their reflections. At length they turned toward shore and, two by two, approached it, unaware of the huntsman who sat motionless among the trees.

But a curious thing happened as the great birds neared the shore: The figures shimmered in the twilight, and when they stepped upon the land, they walked not with the stately waddle of earthbound swans, but with the light tread of young women. They had shed their swan forms, which trailed from their slender fingers as feathered cloaks.

As the hunter watched transfixed, the maidens dropped their cloaks upon the ground and – in a manner as grave and courtly as their swan-swimming – danced. How long the dance lasted or what the music was, the huntsman never afterward could say. When the full moon rose high, silvering the maidens' hair, they gathered up their feathered cloaks and streamed toward the lake. They reached it, and two by two they entered it. As their feet touched the water, the maidens disappeared, and the huntsman saw only pairs of white swans, drifting in the moonlight.

Filled with longing love for the beautiful creatures, the huntsman returned night after night, but a month passed before the moon was full again and the swan flock descended to the lake. Again he watched the maidens' ceremony. This time, however, he stealthily approached them while they were absorbed in the patterns of the dance. As quietly as he could, he drew one feathered cloak from the white pile on the ground.

When the moon was high, the maidens gathered their cloaks and returned to the lake. But the last to leave had no cloak, for hers was the one the huntsman held. She began to search, while her sisters circled anxiously near shore. Then the hunter stepped from the trees, and the swans took wing in a rush of wind. The huntsman was left alone in the moonlight with the swan-maiden. He held out his hand to her. Bowing her head submissively, she took it.

He led the maiden to his house, where he dressed her in mortal women's clothes. In time, he made her his wife. The feathered swan cloak he put away in a locked chest: He wanted the woman, not the swan, but he was afraid to destroy the cloak that transformed her, because it was part of her being.

The swan-woman made a sweet and loving wife. She bore the huntsman a daughter – perfect except for the translucent webs of skin that joined her small toes – and seemed to love that daughter dearly. The huntsman grew accustomed to his wife's silence – she never spoke – and he came to accept her hours of sitting beside the lake where he had found her. She never seemed to tire of gazing at the water. In the spring and autumn, when the wing music of migrating swans sounded above the house, the wife's eyes filled with tears, and the hunter comforted her as best he could with mortal love.

Thus the years passed peacefully enough, and the huntsman half-forgot the swan cloak. The day came at last when he opened the chest and saw it once more. His wife saw it, too, but she, of course, said nothing. She drew her small daughter into her arms, however, and watched while her husband locked the chest and put away the key.

Coils of a serpent bride

Chroniclers of the elder days tell of fairy creatures called lamias who appeared in numerous threatening guises – as monstrous serpents, for instance, or as scaled and clawed beasts. But lamias were perhaps most dangerous when they walked abroad as beautiful women. Although their natures were amorous and haunted by a yearning love for mortals, the lamias represented the darkest side of Faerie.

Near Corinth once, a young man named Lycius came upon a woman of such glowing beauty and sinuous charm that his heart was captured instantly. She gazed at him with adoration, and before long, the woman became the young man's mistress. Their hours together were so full of joy that Lycius determined to marry her.

He arranged a splendid wedding feast. But at the height of the festivities, he saw that his bride was pale and almost swooning. She trembled ceaselessly where she stood, and her breath came in hissing sighs. As he went to her aid, she gestured dumbly at an aged man who stood among the guests. That man was Lycius' mentor, a philosopher who had guided him faithfully. His gaze was fixed on the bride, and his expression was grim.

At length the wise one turned to Lycius and said, "I will not see you made a serpent's prey. You will die in this creature's coils."

A howl of pain tore through the crowded chamber. The woman writhed, and then, in the spot where she had stood, the guests saw a shimmer of sapphire and gold and green – the scales of a jewel-like snake. An instant later, the bride had vanished.

The philosopher had recognized the fairy threat too late, however. Bereft of his love, Lycius died. His marriage robe became his winding sheet.

The swan-wife left at the next full moon. The huntsman returned home to find the fire out, the house cold and his daughter playing alone on the floor beside the treasure chest, whose lid was open and whose interior was empty. At that moment, he heard the wing music of the swans, and when he carried his daughter to the door, he saw the flock overhead. The great white birds circled above the house, then headed away.

The huntsman lived alone with his daughter for the rest of his life. He never married, for no mortal could match his swan wife. And though he watched and waited patiently for years, he never saw the enchanted flock again.

The swan fairy gave the huntsman love for love, in her gentle fashion. But she was a wild creature taken by capture. Out of her element in the world of mortals, she always pined for her own kind.

It was often so with the wilder elves. A tale was told in Shropshire of a knight who paid through many a long year for his capture of a fairy bride. His name was Edric and his story was this:

Edric rode out hunting one afternoon and lost his way in a wood. Night fell, and he rode on in the darkness for hours. Finally, he came upon a palace, ablaze with festive lights. Through the windows he saw dancing maidens, taller and more lovely than any mortal maid could be, and one of them taller and lovelier than the rest. Edric, overcome with passion, burst into the palace and tore her from the ranks of her sisters, although they fought him as best they could.

In the morning, Edric rode home with his prize. But not all of his wooing could gain a look or word from her. Three days passed. At last the fairy turned to him and said, "You have captured me for a wife, and I must bide with you. But if you once name my sisters or the place that I come from, I will have my freedom and you will lose your fortune and your life."

So the fairy captive stayed with Edric as his wife. She vanished from time to time, and the mortal bore this as patiently as he could, for she always returned. One day, however, jealous of her absence, Edric reproached his wife, crying that her love for her elvish sisters was greater than what she owed her husband.

She vanished at once, as she had warned him she would, to rejoin her fairy kind. But it was said that when Edric died— which he soon did—she returned to claim his soul. Condemned to a restless existence in Faerie forever afterward, he periodically led an armed host through the English countryside, and people who saw that company called it a portent of war.

Some fairies were less attached to their own world than Edric's bride. They loved mortals of their own free will and could be wooed and won. Nonetheless, conditions were imposed upon these marriages—conditions that served, like the symbolic rituals in the marriages between unrelated mortals, to emphasize the alien character of man and wife. A mortal man who married a fairy woman, for example, might be forbidden to touch her with iron—always an anathema to fairies, for reasons no one knew—or, as with Edric's wife, to speak of her fairy origin, or to strike her, even lightly. And these conditions were no mere symbols. They were charged with power. The fairy's continued stay in the mortal world depended on the rigorous observation of them.

A lord of the castle of Argouges in France, for instance, loved a fairy who loved him in return and agreed to marry him, provided only that he never mention the word "death" in her presence. This seemed an easy task, and the union was a happy one that lasted for many years and produced handsome children. One day, however, the fairy — who seems to have been somewhat frivolous — lingered long over her dressing. When, at length, she appeared in the great hall of the castle, her irritated husband snapped out a common proverb. "Madam," he said, "You would be a fine messenger to summon Death, for you take a long time to finish your business." At the word, his pretty wife wailed and disappeared. Her husband found no trace of her ever again, save for the print of her hand on the castle gate.

It was ever thus. The price of love that spanned two worlds — small as that price might be — seemed greater than mortals could pay. Even so, the joys of that love, however brief, were remembered for centuries, as a Welsh tale tells.

Near the Black Mountains of that country was a small lake called Llyn y Fan Fach. A farmer of the region used to graze his cattle close to its shores. Early one morning, he saw a strange sight indeed. A gleam of gold shone through the mist on the wa-ter's surface. As the sun rose and the mist burned away, the gleam became a real image. Sitting lightly on the surface of the water was a beautiful young woman. Head bent so that she could use the water as a looking glass, she was combing her golden hair. The farmer made a movement, and the maiden looked up at once. When she saw the tall young man on the bank, she gave a smile of piercing sweetness.

The farmer was enchanted. He knew her for a *gwraig annwfn*, a lake fairy who, unlike the dangerous water spirits of other countries, was full of affection for mortals. Heart pounding and hands trembling — for her beauty was unearthly — the farmer stretched out his hands and entreated her to cross the water to him. He offered her the only gift he had to give — a loaf of bread, the staff of mortal life.

She shook her head. "Your bread is too hard," said the fairy. But she smiled once more upon him before she sank into the lake, leaving only a golden nimbus on the water to mark the place where she had disappeared.

The farmer returned the following day and found the fairy drifting gently just above the ripples of the lake. He bore a loaf of unbaked bread dough, but this she would not take, saying it was too soft, and she sank once more beneath the surface.

The third day, the farmer brought the proper offering for a fairy: a lightly baked loaf that, being neither raw nor fully cooked, partook of the mystery of borderlines and of all things that escaped definition. The surface of the lake was empty when he arrived, but when he held out his gift, there rose from the depths of the wa-

An elfin champion

If the old tales are true, there once lived fairies whose task was the defense of undefended humans. These beings, both brave and loving, sometimes married mortals, yet even for them, the way between the worlds was doomed by human frailty. So it was with the Knight of the Swan.

In Flanders, an orphaned heiress named Elsam was put in the charge of a knight whose name was Telramund. Being a man of ambition and little scruple, Telramund sought to marry his ward and thus acquire her lands. He claimed that she had promised him her hand. She steadily denied this and steadily refused him.

At length the matter was brought before the German Emperor at Antwerp. He decreed that it should be settled in trial by combat: Telramund was to battle Elsam's champion – if anyone chose to assume that role.

At that moment, in the Castle of the Grail, far away on the enchanted island of Monsalvach, bells began to chime. Knights conferred together. Then one of them began a journey.

On the appointed day, the court assembled by the Scheldt River. The herald called for a champion. As the sound of his trumpet died, a boat drawn by a swan swept up the river. It had come from Monsalvach and it bore a knight to defend the maid. All afternoon, steel rang against steel as the Knight of the Swan and Telramund battled. At last the elf sent the mortal crashing to the ground.

Elsam married her savior and loved him well for many years. Yet he was a stranger still, for the condition of the marriage was that she never seek to know her husband's origins. At last, however, she asked about his lineage. Sadly he turned from her and sighed. He took her to the banks of the Scheldt River, and there he told her of the Castle of the Grail. As he spoke, the swan-drawn craft appeared. The knight stepped into it and, leaning on his shield, stared ahead at the curving river as the boat carried him out of Elsam's life forever.

ter a tall old man with a flowing beard. He was flanked by two golden maidens.

The old man regarded the farmer impassively and said, "You may have the maiden you desire, if you can tell me which of my daughters is she."

This was like the riddle trials sometimes held before mortal weddings, but infinitely harder, for the young women who stood before the farmer were as alike as two peas.

He studied them, searching for a clue. He looked at their hair and their faces and their flowing gowns and found them exactly the same. His glance dropped to the surface of the water, where the hems of their skirts rippled. From the skirts of one maiden peeped two small shoes. The farmer recognized them and made his choice.

There was a pause.

"You have chosen well," the old man said at last. "That is the maiden you love, and you may take her to wife. But treat her kindly. If you strike her as many as three causeless blows, I will have her back with me." The farmer gave his word that he would cherish his wife, and the old man sank into the water, taking with him the *gwraig annwfn's* sister.

Light as a dragonfly, the *gwraig annwfn* skipped across the water and onto the shore. She ran straight into the farmer's arms, smiling her sweet smile.

So the two were married, and they were happy indeed. As the years passed, the fairy bore her husband three fine sons, who in later life became physicians of otherworldly and intuitive skill.

But the *gwraig annwfn* had curious ways, and these disturbed her husband, happy as he was with her. She fell sometimes into trances and sometimes conversed with beings he could not see. And she did other things as well.

The couple went to the christening of a neighbor's child, and the *gwraig annwfn* wept throughout. To a fairy, a christening was a sad occasion: The conferral of a mortal name severed a human's inborn ties with the other world. But the farmer did not understand this, and in his shame at her behavior, he rebuked her with the lightest of taps on the arm.

"That is the first blow," was all the *gwraig annwfn* said.

They went together to a wedding, and while those about her were joyful, the fairy wept. They went to a funeral, where she laughed. She understood that sadness and joy could go hand in hand on any occasion, and she lacked the fear of censure that governed much of mortal behavior. But her husband understood only that his wife had shamed him. After the wedding, he railed at her for weeping, and then he struck her.

"That is the second blow," the fairy said. "Take heed how you treat me if you would keep me." But again the husband forgot, and when the funeral was over, he struck her once more.

"That is the third blow," said the fairy wife. "Now I must go to my home in the lake." And she wept with sadness as she looked for the last time on the husband who had betrayed her.

The farmer understood then what he had done and what he must pay. Tears coursed down his cheeks as he watched the fairy leave his house and cross the meadows to the lake where he had found her.

The Secret Suitor

Breton singers told of an elfin knight and a mortal whose love remained steadfast through both joy and woe. Once, went the tale, there lived a rich and mean-spirited lord whose chief pleasure was in the hunt and the kill. In his old age he sought a wife. His gold bought him one of good family, a maiden so tender and gay that the lord shut her in a tower and set a guard upon her, lest she attract admirers younger and more ardent than he.

For seven years the young wife languished, alone save for the visits of her wardens and of her aged spouse. No child was born of the unhappy union, and she pined and drooped and faded.

She dreamed wistfully, in her solitude, of the ladies of her father's court with their dashing chevaliers, and she longed for one who would love her as they were loved. At last one morning, when the sunlight lay in bars across the chamber, she wished aloud for a lover to warm her cold prison. Through the window came a rush of wind, and a moment later, a falcon settled on the sill. As the lady gazed at the bird, it faded into the bright air. She closed her eyes, then opened them to see the fairest of men standing before her. "Do not fear me, Lady," he said gently. He told her that in another country he was a Prince. He said he had seen her long ago and had loved her, and he explained that the wish she had uttered had let him come to her. The lady's heart flew out to him.

From then on, she summoned the Prince when she could, and he came to her from his country. In those days of her passion, she bloomed as sweetly as a rose.

But the old lord saw her happiness, and he set spies upon her. When they told him of the falcon-prince, he devised a trap. Before the next dawn, the lady called her lover. She heard the rush of wings and then a cry: The great bird, bleeding profusely, lay pinioned on spikes concealed within the window frame. At last the falcon wrenched itself free and, barely able to stay aloft, headed home. Without a thought the lady flung herself from the window—yet the fall did not harm her. She set out to follow the falcon's bloody trail. Now running, now walking, she crossed field and forest until she came to a cavern that pierced a high hill. She entered the darkness and emerged at last to find a fair country of meadows laced with sail-crowded rivers. The trail, she saw, led to a towered city. She walked through the gates and found the streets silent; the people turned aside from her. In the palace was the dying Prince. His eyes brightened when he saw her. He told her that she would bear his son and that the child must be brought up in her own land; to protect her from her husband's wrath, he placed on her finger a ring that would bring the old lord forgetfulness of what had passed. Just before he died, the Prince gave the lady a jeweled sword for their child, who would one day use it to avenge the death of his elfin father.

All happened as the Prince had foretold. Year followed year, and at last the lady's son slew the old lord with the fairy sword his father had left for him. As for the lady, she died of grief.

He saw his wife no more and lived alone the rest of his life, but it was said that while her sons were young, the *gwraig annwfn* visited them and that she disappeared for the last time only after they were grown.

As it was with the lake fairy's husband, so it was with all mortal men – and women, too. The rules that governed elfin marriage always were broken by mortal spouses, through stupidity or curiosity or mistrust or carelessness. It was as if the condition of mortality demanded that sorrow follow joy. And as the history of the fairy Melusine showed, the sorrow engendered by a fairy marriage – unlike its joy – could last from generation to generation.

To relate the tale of Melusine, it is necessary to begin with the fairy's birth and unhappy early life. She was, in fact, just half an elf: Her mother was a fountain fairy named Pressina and her father, named Elinus, was a mortal King of Albany – the ancient name for Scotland. Pressina agreed to marry the King only after he agreed to the elfin condition, which in her case was that he never see her in childbed.

Her husband broke his vow on the day that Pressina gave birth to three beautiful daughters, Melusine, Melior and Plantina. The fairy had to leave him then. Taking her daughters, she fled to a fairy island said to be Avalon.

Years passed, and as the daughters grew, the lonely mother told them of Elinus and his broken vow, and as she spoke she wept for the love she had lost. When the daughters grew into their full powers, they took revenge. They lured their father into a mountain cave in Northumbria, and with a web of spells they closed the cave, so that Elinus remained a prisoner in the dark for the rest of his life.

When Pressina heard what her daughters had done, she wailed with grief and rage, and she set upon them solemn punishments. The fates of the younger daughters, Melior and Plantina, are not important to the story, but that of Melusine – the eldest and the leader – is. Her mother cast this curse: Every Saturday Melusine was condemned to become a loathsome serpent from the waist down, and to stay that way for twenty-four hours. She was doomed, the mother said, not to know the joys of love, unless she could conceal her periodic deformity by finding a lover who would agree not to visit her on the day of her punishment. If that lover agreed to the condition and then broke his word, the mother added, Melusine would spend eternity as a winged snake in perpetual flight – and perpetual pain.

The tale of Melusine's marriage begins in the sun-washed west of France, where the fairy either had fled or had been sent by her mother to guard a forest fountain sometimes called the Fountain of Thirst and sometimes Lusinia. Melusine whiled away the hours there, occasionally attended by forest fairies. For the most part, she bathed in the fountain and sang fairy songs to herself. On Saturdays she retreated into the trees to hide her shameful punishment from any travelers who might chance by.

But none appeared for many months, until at last a young man strode into the clearing. He saw the fountain and heard the sparkling harmonies of its falling water, and at the fountain's edge, half-hidden by leafy shadows, he saw Melusine and heard her wistful, whispered song.

He was charmed by the beautiful maiden. As for the fairy, her heart was captured, and she mourned her ugly secret. But the young man kneeled beside her, stroked her hand and spoke so sweetly that Melusine was calmed. He understood that she was a fountain fairy, and he offered her both heart and hand.

Melusine agreed and, with some hesitation, told him the condition imposed upon them: that he leave her in seclusion each Saturday. (She did not tell the reason.) The young man had a generous and trusting heart, and he gave his word.

According to the chroniclers, that is how the great family of Lusignan was formed: Melusine was to be the forebear of countless counts and kings. For the mortal was Raymond, son of the Earl of Forez. When he married Melusine—and marry they did, in splendid fashion—luck came to him. After the marriage he built the fortress of Lusignan, near Poitou. Some said it was constructed in three nights because of the fairy's aid, but this seems unlikely. Others said it was named for the fairy's fountain, Lusinia, and this is possible.

Whatever the truth, the fortress rose high above its forested mountain, bristling with towers and gleaming with gold. Within were all the pleasures of a palace: The walls were painted in the style called

By a fountain, in a forest in France, the chevalier Raymond came upon the fairies who guarded the place. The loveliest was Melusine, who quickly made his heart her captive.

mille-fleurs, or "thousand flowers," and the archways were hung with tapestries so finely embroidered that only fairies could have made them. Because of the fortress, Raymond was thereafter Lord of Lusignan.

He lived happily with Melusine for many years. She was as light and laughing as the waters of her fountain, and gaiety and good fortune followed her dancing footsteps. Throughout those years, Raymond kept his word: Each Friday just before midnight, he left his wife alone in her tower chamber, returning only when the bells tolled the next midnight.

They had but one grief, and that was their children. Perhaps because of her mother's curse, Melusine bore a succession of malformed children. She brought forth only sons. The first had one eye of red and one of blue—not a great disfigurement, but a sign of otherworldly blood. The second had a face as red as fire; the third had one eye lower than the other.

The next boy was hideously scarred, bearing a mark on his cheek that resembled a lion's claw; and the boy that followed him had only one eye. The sixth child had a tooth like a boar's tusk that protruded from the side of his mouth; he was called Geoffroy au Grand Dent—Geoffrey Great Tooth. He was followed by a brother named Fromont, who had a monstrous brush of hair bristling from his nose, and another brother who had three eyes. The last two children were normal little boys.

But they were small consolation. As Melusine bore son after deformed son, whispers began, first among her women, then in the palace corridors, and finally throughout the countryside. Harsh voices said the fairy blood was destroying the mortal line; others said that Melusine committed adultery on the Saturdays she kept alone, and so brought forth demons.

A loving husband, the Lord of Lusignan discovered his wife's secret, but he said not a word.
The day came, however, when the most brutish of the couple's malformed children murdered
his brother by fire. In his grief, the lord cursed his wife for her serpent nature.

At last, Raymond—despairing of his hideous brood—heeded his kinsmen and broke the vow he had given his wife. He left her, as he always did, at midnight on a Friday, but instead of returning to his own chambers, he concealed himself where he might watch her. This was no difficult task, for Melusine trusted him and therefore was careless of locks and bolts.

What Raymond saw that night filled him with sickness. His wife crept into the bath that awaited her. Her shoulders and arms and breasts were as white and lovely as he knew them, but at her waist the skin roughened and took on a greenish tinge, and below that gleamed the scaly, coiling tail of a serpent. Melusine lounged in the bath all day, heavy lids drooping over glittering eyes. From time to time, a long tongue flicked between the pretty lips and she gave a hungry, hissing sigh.

Raymond left as quietly as he could and said nothing, for he had betrayed the wife he had loved—and he loved her still.

They might have continued this way—Raymond with his secret, Melusine with hers—but for Geoffrey Great Tooth. As brutally vicious as his appearance suggested, Geoffrey crowned a career of murder and pillage by setting fire to the monastery where his brother Fromont had retreated. A hundred monks died.

The news was brought to Raymond as he sat with his wife and courtiers in her chamber. In his despair, he turned on her and cried, "Go, foul snake, contaminator of my children."

Melusine gasped and whitened and swayed. She sank to the floor, and the courtiers gathered around her. When she gained her senses again, her eyes filled with tears at the betrayal. She walked to a window and set her foot on the stone sill. (The footprint, it is said, stayed there for hundreds of years.) With a last glance at her husband, she leaped into the air.

The courtiers clustered at the window, but no body lay in the courtyard below. They waited in silence, and then they heard the howling cry and saw the shining scales of a great winged snake. It circled the tower three times and disappeared.

Raymond stumbled from the room. No one knows if he ever spoke again; he became a hermit and spent his days not on the field of battle or in the courts of the mighty, but in monastic contemplation.

It is said that Melusine flew to Lusignan in secret to nurse her two youngest sons, and that they survived because of her anxious care. No one knew if that was true. But for centuries after, each Friday before the current Lord of Lusignan was to die, a great snake flew wailing around the battle-ments of the palace. In this way, Melusine lived out her mother's punishment.

So, once more, an alien pairing failed to hold. Once more, a marriage between fairy and human ended in tragedy. It would not be the last time. As long as fairies showed themselves in human form, their love was avidly sought. And no wonder: Mortals, bound by rules and beset by mundane woes, saw the hope of immortal happiness in those bright beings, shining with gallantry and grace, and swathed in mystery. The rewards seemed worth the risk. Even at the end of their time, when fairies no longer sought human company, glimpses of them added enchantment to the mortals' measured earth, spinning its stately way through the eternal heavens.

Through a window of the castle of Lusignan flew the fairy Melusine, forever trapped in a serpent's body. But on moonlit nights, it was said, she went back to suckle her children while the castle slept and dreamed.

Trials of a
Charmed Passion

When King Arthur held his court at Caerleon, his restless Queen was apt to cast a wanton eye on the young knights of his company. But a knight named Launfal was proof against the pretty lady's blandishments, although he risked his life in spurning her. His heart was given to a fairy woman, whom he had met in a woodland, at a time when he was out of favor with the court because of his poverty.

The encounter happened this way. Alone and melancholy, Launfal had ridden deep into the forest one midsummer's day. At length he dismounted, flung himself down on a grassy bank and closed his eyes to the sunshine. After a while, the murmur of sweet voices roused him. Nearby were two golden-haired maidens, who signaled to him. He arose and followed the maids through the trees to a clearing ablaze with wild flowers, where he saw a pavilion of embroidered silk, adorned with gilded roses and crowned with an eagle of burnished gold. It sheltered a maiden who was so radiant that

every memory of mortal beauty faded from Launfal's mind.

She welcomed him sweetly and gave him her hand. At her touch, love kindled between the two. Launfal asked that she stay with him always, but this was not possible, the lady said: He was a mortal and she a fairy. She could appear whenever he wished for her, she said, but only on certain conditions. He must never speak of her (no small sacrifice, in a day when knights dedicated every deed to a lady), and he must not summon her at a time when other mortals were present. If her existence was revealed, she would disappear forever to her own distant lands. Fittingly, her name was Tryamour, which meant "test of love."

Launfal agreed to her terms, and all that long afternoon they remained together in the sunny clearing. When next he appeared at Caerleon, he seemed a different man. He was richly dressed and bravely armed, and he rode a magnificent charger. He kept alone in his chambers at night, when Tryamour came to him; but by day he shone with happiness. The Queen did not fail to notice this, and from time to time her gray eyes rested on him reflectively. She said little, but at length she summoned Launfal.

He found the Queen in a dark and high-walled palace garden. She quickly came to the point: He had become her heart's desire; she wished to make him her paramour. Unmoved,

Launfal courteously refused. The Queen cried, "You are no man fit for a woman's love."

"Queen," said Launfal, "I am beloved of a lady whose lowliest handmaiden puts your beauty to shame."

It was an insult, of course, but it was worse than that. Launfal had revealed the existence of his lover and thereby closed the gate that had opened between the mortal realm and that of Faerie. Tossing her jeweled braids and trailing threats, Guinevere strode from the garden. Launfal secluded himself in his chamber and mourned. He had betrayed Tryamour. When he called, there was no answer.

Presently, mailed fists drummed at his door. Launfal was bound and taken before King Arthur, for reasons that soon became clear. Guinevere had told the King that his knight had tried to force her love, that she had refused and that he had insulted her with the beauty of his mistress.

The penalty for the double infraction was death. But Arthur's knights looked doubtful when they heard the Queen's tale, for her amorous habits were well known to them. They supported Launfal, and in the end he was asked only to produce his mistress within the year, that all might judge her beauty against that of the Queen. This, of course, Launfal could not do. Thus the day came when he stood in the palace courtyard, head bowed, arms bound, awaiting death by fire.

But before the pyre was set alight, a cool breeze stirred in the stifling stillness. It carried the scent of wild flowers. Through the gate on a white palfrey rode Tryamour. Her hair was a halo of gold, her cheeks were softly flushed and her body was as quick and bright as a sunbeam. She smiled upon Launfal and, without speaking a word, turned to the King and court. All were silent.

King Arthur spoke at last: "If you are Launfal's lady," said he, "there is no one who can deny that he spoke truth. He may go free."

So his fellow knights released their brother from his bonds. Without a backward glance, Sir Launfal strode across the courtyard to the lady from the realm of Faerie and leaped up behind her on the white horse. Launfal and Tryamour rode together out of the castle gates and into the meadow beyond, dwindling in the distance and finally vanishing.

Tryamour was never seen again. It was said that she had taken her lover far across the seas to live on the fairy island of Avalon, from which she never could return. But Launfal reappeared in the forests near Caerleon once each year on the eve of the day he had left. A shadowy figure in the fading light of dusk, he was mounted on a splendid charger, and he rode alone, a hint of longing on his face for the mortal world that he had forsaken.

Bibliography

Andersen, Hans Christian, *Stories from Hans Andersen*. New York: Abaris Books, 1979.

Anderson, Janice, and Edmund Swinglehurst, *Scottish Walks and Legends: The Lowlands and East Scotland*. London: Granada Publishing, 1982.

*Arrowsmith, Nancy, with George Moorse, *A Field Guide to the Little People*. New York: Pocket Books, 1978.

Basile, Giovanni Batiste, *Il Pentamerone*. Transl. by Sir Richard Burton. New York: Boni & Liveright, 1927.

Benwell, Gwen, and Arthur Waugh, *Sea Enchantress: The Tale of the Mermaid and Her Kin*. New York: The Citadel Press, 1965.

Blinoff, Marthe, *Life and Thought in Old Russia*. The Pennsylvania State University, 1961.

Boucher, Alan; transl., *Elves, Trolls and Elemental Beings: Icelandic Folktales*, Vol. 2. Reykjavik: Iceland Review, 1977.

Briggs, Katharine:
Abbey Lubbers, Banshees & Boggarts: An Illustrated Encyclopedia of Fairies. New York: Pantheon, 1979.
A Dictionary of British Folk-Tales in the English Language. London: Routledge & Kegan Paul, 1970.
An Encyclopedia of Fairies: Hobgoblins, Brownies, Bogies, and Other Supernatural Creatures. New York: Pantheon, 1976.
The Fairies in English Tradition and Literature. Chicago: The University of Chicago Press, 1967.
The Personnel of Fairyland. Detroit: Singing Tree Press, 1971. (Reprint of 1953 edition.)
The Vanishing People: Fairy Lore and Legends. New York: Pantheon, 1978.

Bringsværd, Tor Age, *Phantoms and Fairies from Norwegian Folklore*. Transl. by Pat Shaw Iversen. Oslo: Johan Grundt Tanum Forlag, no date.

*Cavendish, Richard, ed., *Man, Myth & Magic*. 11 vols. New York: Marshall Cavendish, 1983.

*Child, Francis James, ed., *The English and Scottish Popular Ballads*, Vol. 1. New York: Pageant, 1956.

Craigie, William A., ed. and transl., *Scandinavian Folk-Lore*. Detroit: Singing Tree Press, 1970.

Croker, Thomas Crofton, *Fairy Legends and Traditions of the South of Ireland*. London: John Murray, 1825.

Curtin, Jeremiah, *Tales of the Fairies and of the Ghost World*. New York: Benjamin Blom, 1971. (Reprint of 1895 edition.)

D'Arbois de Jubainville, H., *The Irish Mythological Cycle and Celtic Mythology*. Transl. by Richard Irvine Best. Dublin: Hodges, Figgis & Co., 1903.

*Edwards, Gillian, *Hobgoblin and Sweet Puck: Fairy Names and Natures*. London: Geoffrey Bles, 1974.

*Evans-Wentz, W. Y., *The Fairy-Faith in Celtic Countries*. Secaucus, New Jersey: University Books, 1966.

Folkard, Richard, Jr., *Plant-Lore, Legends and Lyrics*. London: Sampson Low, Marston, Searle, and Rivington, 1884.

Folklore, Myths and Legends of Britain. London: The Reader's Digest Association, 1973.

Ford, Patrick K., transl., *The Mabinogi and Other Medieval Welsh Tales*. Berkeley: University of California Press, 1977.

Gantz, Jeffrey, transl., *Early Irish Myths and Sagas*. Harmondsworth, Middlesex, England: Penguin, 1982.

Gill, W. Walter, *A Second Manx Scrapbook*. London: Arrowsmith, 1932.

Graves, Robert, ed., *English and Scottish Ballads*. London: Heinemann, 1957.

*Gregory, Lady, transl., *Gods and Fighting Men*. 2nd ed. New York: Oxford University Press, 1970.

Grimm, Jacob, *Teutonic Mythology*, Vol. 1. Transl. by James Steven Stallybrass. Gloucester, Massachusetts: Peter Smith, 1976.

Haining, Peter, *The Leprechaun's Kingdom*. New York: Harmony Books, 1980.

*Hanning, Robert, and Joan Ferrante, transls., *The Lais of Marie de France*. New York: E. P. Dutton, 1978.

*Hartland, Edwin Sidney, *The Science of Fairy Tales: An Inquiry into Fairy Mythology*. New York: Scribner & Welford, 1891.

*Hastings, James, ed., *Encyclopaedia of Religion and Ethics*, Vol. 5. Edinburgh: T. & T. Clark, 1912.

Henderson, William, *Notes on the Folk-Lore of the Northern Counties of England and the Borders*. London: W. Satchell, Peyton, 1879.

Hunt, Robert, ed., *Popular Romances of the West of England: or Drolls, Traditions, and Superstitions of Old Cornwall*. 3rd ed. London: Chatto and Windus, 1881.

*Keightley, Thomas, *The Fairy Mythology*. London: Wildwood House, 1981. (Reprint of 1892 edition.)

Kirk, Robert, *The Secret Commonwealth of Elves, Fauns and Fairies*. 3rd ed. Stirling, Scotland: Eneas Mackay, 1933. (Original ms., 1691.)

*Leach, Maria, ed., *Funk & Wagnalls Standard Dictionary of Folklore, Mythology and Legend*. New York: Funk & Wagnalls, 1949.

MacCulloch, John Arnott, *The Mythology of All Races*, Vol. 2, *Eddic*. New York: Cooper Square Publishers, 1964.

*MacCulloch, John Arnott, and Jan Machal, *The Mythology of All Races*, Vol. 3, *Celtic, Slavic*. New York: Cooper Square Publishers, 1964.

Mackenzie, Donald A., *Scottish Folk-Lore and Folk Life: Studies in Race, Culture and Tradition*. London: Blackie & Son, 1935.

Mason, Eugene, transl., *French Mediaeval Romances from the Lays of Marie de France*. London: J. M.

Dent & Sons, 1976. (Reprint of 1924 edition.)

Maxym, Lucy, *Russian Lacquer, Legends and Fairy Tales.* Manhasset, New York: Siamese Imports, 1981.

O'Grady, Standish H., ed. and transl., *Silva Gadelica: A Collection of Tales in Irish.* London: Williams and Norgate, 1892.

Paton, Lucy Allen, *Studies in the Fairy Mythology of Arthurian Romance.* 2nd ed. New York: Burt Franklin, 1960.

Phillpotts, Beatrice, *The Book of Fairies.* New York: Ballantine Books, 1979.

Porteous, Alexander, *Forest Folklore; Mythology, and Romance.* Detroit: Singing Tree Press, 1968. (Reprint of 1928 edition.)

Ralston, W. R. S., *Russian Folk-Tales.* London: Smith, Elder, 1873.

*Rees, Alwyn and Brinley, *Celtic Heritage: Ancient Tradition in Ireland and Wales.* New York: Thames and Hudson, 1961.

Rickert, Edith, transl., *Early English Romances in Verse.* New York: Cooper Square Publishers, 1966.

Robinson, Herbert Spencer, and Knox Wilson, *Myths and Legends of All Nations.* New York: Garden City Publishing, 1950.

Rolleston, T. W., *Myths & Legends of the Celtic Race.* New York: Lemma Publishing, 1974. (Reprint of 1934 edition.)

Rossetti, Christina, *Goblin Market.* New York: Franklin Watts, 1969.

Shakespeare, William, *Shakespeare, Complete Works.* Ed. by W. J. Craig. Oxford University Press, 1980.

Sikes, Wirt, *British Goblins: Welsh Folk-Lore, Fairy Mythology, Legends and Traditions.* Wakefield, Yorkshire, England: EP Publishing, 1973. (Reprint of 1880 edition.)

Sjoestedt, Marie-Louise, *Gods and Heroes of the Celts.* Transl. by Myles Dillon. London: Methuen, 1949.

Spence, Lewis:
British Fairy Origins. Wellingborough, Northamptonshire, England: The Aquarian Press, 1981.
The Fairy Tradition in Britain. London: Rider, 1948.

Stephens, James, *Irish Fairy Tales.* New York: Abaris Books, 1978.

Tongue, Ruth L., comp., *Forgotten Folk-Tales of the English Counties.* London: Routledge & Kegan Paul, 1970.

Tudor-Craig, Sir Algernon Tudor, comp., *The Romance of Melusine and de Lusignan.* London: The Century House, 1932.

Ward, Donald, ed. and transl., *The German Legends of the Brothers Grimm,* Vol. 2. Philadelphia: Institute for the Study of Human Issues, 1981.

*Wilde, Lady Francesca, *Ancient Legends, Mystic Charms & Superstitions of Ireland.* London: Chatto & Windus, 1925.

Wilson, Barbara Ker, ed., *Scottish Folk-Tales and Legends.* London: Oxford University Press, 1954.

Yeats, W. B., ed., *Fairy and Folk Tales of Ireland.* London: Pan Books, 1979.

Titles marked with an asterisk were especially helpful in the preparation of this volume.

Picture Credits

Blauel/Artothek, Munich. 58: Artwork by Wayne Anderson. 60, 61: J. W. Waterhouse, City of Manchester Art Gallery, courtesy The Bridgeman Art Library, London. 63: Reproduced from *Russian Lacquer, Legends and Fairy Tales* by Lucy Maxym, © Siamese Imports Co., Inc. 64: Edmund Dulac, copyright Geraldine M. Anderson, from *Stories from Hans Andersen,* Hodder and Stoughton, 1911, courtesy Mary Evans Picture Library, London. 65, 66: Artwork by Wayne Anderson. 68-75: Artwork by Kinuko Y. Craft. 76, 77: Artwork by Thomas Woodruff. 79: Sir Edward Burne-Jones, courtesy Hammersmith & Fulham Public Libraries,

photographed by Derek Bayes, London. 80-84: Artwork by Winslow Pinney Pels. 85: E. R. Hughes, courtesy Sotheby Parke Bernet & Co., London. 87: Artwork by Wayne Anderson. 88, 89: Sir Joseph Noel Paton, courtesy Glasgow Museums and Art Galleries, Glasgow. 90, 91: Artwork by Winslow Pinney Pels. 92, 93: Artwork by Rallé. 94, 95: Artwork by Winslow Pinney Pels. 96, 97: Sir Joseph Noel Paton, Roy Miles Fine Paintings, courtesy The Bridgeman Art Library, London. 98: Artwork by Winslow Pinney Pels. 99: Arthur Rackham, from *Goblin Market* by C. G. Rossetti, George G. Harrap & Co. Ltd., London, 1933, by per-

mission of Barbara Edwards. 100-107: Artwork by Jill Karla Schwarz. 108, 109: Sir Frank Dicksee, City of Bristol Museum and Art Gallery, courtesy The Bridgeman Art Library, London. 113: Reproduced from *Russian Lacquer, Legends and Fairy Tales* by Lucy Maxym, © Siamese Imports Co., Inc. 114, 115: Artwork by Dennis Luzak. 117: J. W. Waterhouse, private collection, photographed by Derek Bayes, London. 120, 121: Artwork by James C. Christensen. 123-126: Artwork by Alicia Austin. 128-131: Photo Bibliothèque Nationale, Paris. 132-139: Artwork by Kinuko Y. Craft. 144: Artwork by Józef Sumichrast.

Acknowledgments

The editors are particularly indebted to John Dorst, consultant, for his help in the preparation of this volume. The editors also wish to thank the following persons and institutions: François Avril, Curator, Département des Manuscrits, Bibliothèque Nationale, Paris; Stella Beddoe, Art Gallery and Museum, Brighton, England; M. Begg, National Library of Scotland, Edinburgh; Mary Bennett, Keeper of British Art, Walker Art Gallery, Liverpool; Barbara Blank, New York City; Jean-Loup Charmet, Paris; Christopher Wood Gallery, London; Ann Cruikshank, Professor of Fine Art, Trinity College, Dublin; Anne Donald, Keeper of Fine Art, Glasgow; Dr. Michael Droller, Baltimore; Frances Dunkels, Department of Prints and Drawings, British Museum, London; Clark Evans, Rare Book and Special Collections Division, Library of Congress, Washington, D.C.; Hillary Evans, London; Mary Evans, London; Antonio Faeti, Bologna, Italy; Folk-Lore Society, London; Henry Ford, Maas Gallery, London; Martin Forrest, Bourne Fine Art, Edin-

burgh; Jacqueline Fowler, Stamford, Connecticut; Marielise Göpel, Archiv für Kunst und Geschichte, West Berlin; Francis Greenacre, Curator of Fine Art, City of Bristol Museum and Art Gallery, England; Jocelyn Grigg, Curator, Mackintosh Collection, Glasgow School of Art, Scotland; Robin Gwyndaf, Welsh Folk Museum, Cardiff; Michael Heseltine, Sotheby Parke Bernet and Co., London; Anthony Hobson, Moreton Morrell, England; Christine Hoffman, Bayerische Staatsgemäldesammlungen, Munich; Brian Kennedy, Ulster Museum, Belfast; Heidi Klein, Bildarchiv Preussischer Kulturbesitz, West Berlin; Lionel Lambourne, Victoria and Albert Museum, London; Françoise Lemmonier, Bibliothéque Nationale, Paris; Sheila MacGregor, Keeper of Fine Art, Atkinson Art Gallery, Southport, England; Alister Matthews, Bournemouth, England; C. Lloyd Morgan, National Library of Wales, Cardiff; Alice Munro-Faure, Sotheby Parke Bernet and Co., London; Maureen Park, Glasgow Art Gallery and Museum,

Scotland; Beatrice Phillpotts, London; Christine Poulson, London; Walt Reed, Illustration House, South Norwalk, Connecticut; Jo Ann Reisler, Vienna, Virginia; Michel Rival, Bibliothèque Nationale, Paris; R. A. Saunders, Keeper of Art, Paisley Art Gallery, Scotland; Justin Schiller, New York City; Lawrence Seeborg, Greenbelt, Maryland; Robert Shields, Rare Book and Special Collections Division, Library of Congress, Washington, D.C.; Tessa Sidey, Birmingham Museum and Art Gallery, England; Peyton Skipwith, Fine Art Society, London; South Africa National Gallery, Cape Town; Soviet Copyright Agency, Moscow; Hugh Stevenson, Glasgow Art Gallery and Museum, Scotland; Wiebke Tomaschek, Staatliche Graphische Sammlung, Munich; Leonie von Wilkins, Germanisches Nationalmuseum, Nuremberg; Stephen Wildman, Birmingham Museum and Art Gallery, England; R. Williams, Department of Prints and Drawings, British Museum, London; Michael Wynne, Keeper, National Gallery of Ireland, Dublin.

Time-Life Books Inc.
is a wholly owned subsidiary of

TIME INCORPORATED

FOUNDER: Henry R. Luce 1898-1967

Editor-in-Chief: Henry Anatole Grunwald
President: J. Richard Munro
Chairman of the Board: Ralph P. Davidson
Corporate Editor: Jason McManus
Group Vice President, Books: Reginald K. Brack Jr.

TIME-LIFE BOOKS INC.

EDITOR: George Constable
Executive Editor: George Daniels
Director of Design: Louis Klein
Editorial Board: Roberta Conlan, Ellen
Phillips, Gerry Schremp, Gerald Simons,
Rosalind Stubenberg, Kit van Tulleken,
Henry Woodhead
Editorial General Manager: Neal Goff
Director of Research: Phyllis K. Wise
Director of Photography: John Conrad Weiser

PRESIDENT: Reginald K. Brack Jr.
Senior Vice President: William Henry
Vice Presidents: George Artandi, Stephen L.
Bair, Robert A. Ellis, Juanita T. James,
Christopher T. Linen, James L. Mercer,
Joanne A. Pello, Paul R. Stewart

THE ENCHANTED WORLD

SERIES DIRECTOR: Ellen Phillips
Deputy Editor: Robin Richman
Designer: Dale Pollekoff
Chief Researcher: Jane Edwin

Editorial Staff for *Fairies and Elves*
Text Editors: Tim Appenzeller,
Richard Murphy
Researchers: Charlotte Marine Fullerton,
(principal), Patricia N. McKinney
Assistant Designer: Lorraine D. Rivard
Copy Coordinators: Anthony K. Pordes,
Barbara Fairchild Quarmby
Picture Coordinator: Nancy C. Scott
Editorial Assistant: Constance B. Strawbridge

Special Contributor: Martha Reichard George

Editorial Operations
Design: Ellen Robling (assistant director)
Copy Room: Diane Ullius
Production: Anne B. Landry (director),
Celia Beattie
Quality Control: James J. Cox (director),
Sally Collins
Library: Louise D. Forstall

Correspondents: Elisabeth Kraemer-Singh
(Bonn); Margot Hapgood, Dorothy Bacon
(London); Miriam Hsia, Lucy T. Voulgaris
(New York); Maria Vincenza Aloisi,
Josephine du Brusle (Paris); Ann Natanson
(Rome). Valuable assistance was also
provided by: Angelika Lemmer (Bonn);
Lois Lorimer (Copenhagen); Peter
Hawthorne (Johannesburg); Lesley Coleman
(London); Felix Rosenthal (Moscow);
Carolyn T. Chubet (New York); Bent
Onsager (Oslo); Eva Stichova (Prague);
Phoebe Natanson, Ann Wise (Rome); Mary
Johnson (Stockholm).

Chief Series Consultant

Tristram Potter Coffin, Professor of
English at the University of Pennsylvania, is a leading authority on folklore.
He is the author or editor of numerous
books and more than one hundred arti-
cles. His best-known works are *The British Traditional Ballad in North America*, *The
Old Ball Game*, *The Book of Christmas Folk-
lore* and *The Female Hero*.

This volume is one of a series based
on myths, legends and folk tales.

Other Publications:

THE KODAK LIBRARY OF CREATIVE PHOTOGRAPHY
GREAT MEALS IN MINUTES
THE CIVIL WAR
PLANET EARTH
COLLECTOR'S LIBRARY OF THE CIVIL WAR
LIBRARY OF HEALTH
CLASSICS OF THE OLD WEST
THE EPIC OF FLIGHT
THE GOOD COOK
THE SEAFARERS
WORLD WAR II
HOME REPAIR AND IMPROVEMENT
THE OLD WEST
LIFE LIBRARY OF PHOTOGRAPHY (revised)
LIFE SCIENCE LIBRARY (revised)

For information on and a full description of
any of the Time-Life Books series listed
above, please write:
Reader Information
Time-Life Books
541 North Fairbanks Court
Chicago, Illinois 60611

Library of Congress Cataloguing in
Publication Data
Fairies and elves.
(The Enchanted world)
Bibliography: p.
1. Fairies.   I. Time-Life Books.
II. Title.   III. Series.
GR549.F35 1984   398.2'1   84-186
ISBN 0-8094-5212-X
ISBN 0-8094-5213-8 (lib. bdg.)

Time-Life Books Inc. offers a wide range of
fine recordings, including a *Big Bands* series.
For subscription information, call 1-800-621-
7026, or write TIME-LIFE MUSIC, Time &
Life Building, Chicago, Illinois 60611.

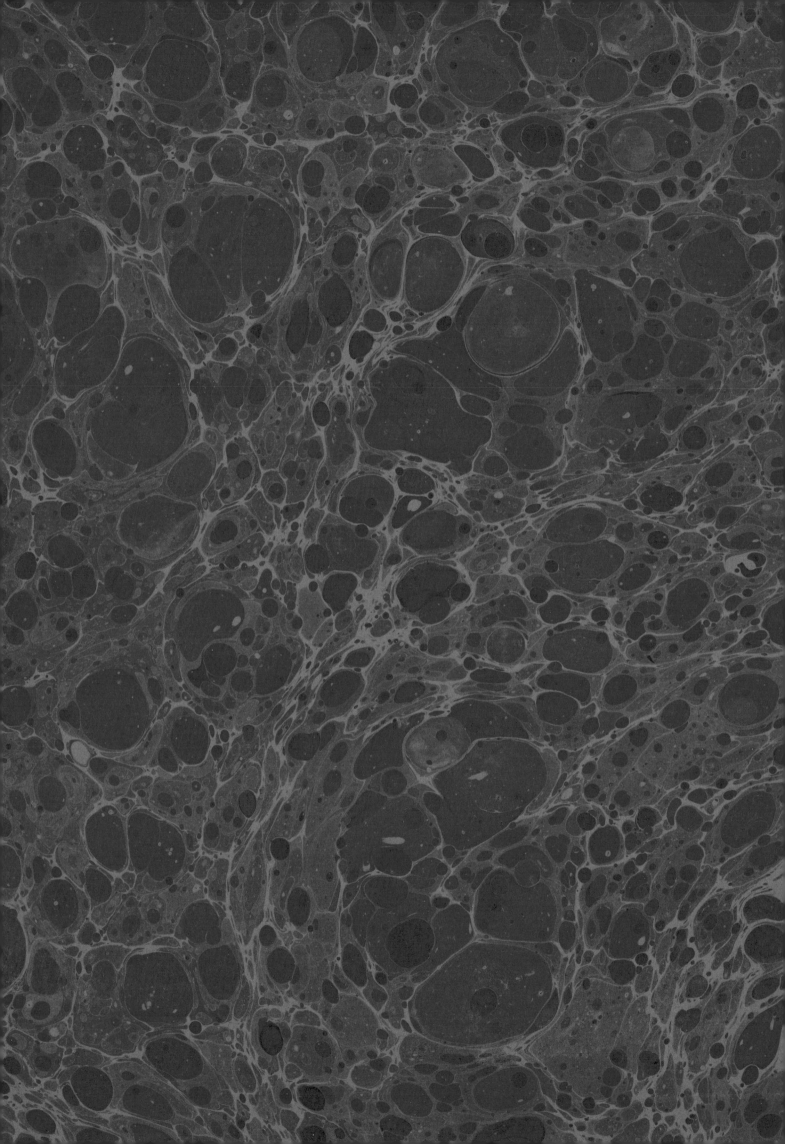